Changing Purchasing tov

Changing Purchasing towards Procurement 4.0

Digitalization in Procurement. Understand Procurement processes and how the most hidden important department can drive towards the future. AI, Blockchain, Lean methods, and much more are presented to implement real change. Redefining Procurement.

Dennis Roßbach

Bibliografische Information der Deutschen Nationalbibliothek
Die Deutsche Nationalbibliothek verzeichnet diese Publikation in der
Deutschen Nationalbibliografie; detaillierte bibliographische Daten sind im
Internet über http://dnb.d-nb.de abrufbar.
1. Aufl. - Göttingen: Cuvillier, 2022

© CUVILLIER VERLAG, Göttingen 2022
Nonnenstieg 8, 37075 Göttingen
Telefon: 0551-54724-0
Telefax: 0551-54724-21
www.cuvillier.de

1. Auflage, 2022
Gedruckt auf umweltfreundlichem, säurefreiem Papier aus nachhaltiger Forst-
wirtschaft.

ISBN 978-3-7369-7522-4
eISBN 978-3-7369-6522-5

To my parents

PROLOGUE

Because Procurement and Purchasing and the supply chain are crucial in today's fast-changing world, this book gives you a comprehensive overview of what Procurement and Purchasing are. The focus lies on Procurement 4.0 and what the future will provide to us all in this work area, not only for Procurement professionals but also for everyone who wants to deepen their knowledge on this important topic. Every company procures goods and services. Learn how you can adapt your processes to the future and learn more about new technologies like Blockchain, AI, Robotic Process Automation, and many more.

Agile methods are tied together with all these processes, and we will look at Lean principles as well. In the end, you will learn how you can set up a smart contract with Ethereum.

Get future-ready and let's "Redefine Procurement".

Luxembourg, 2021 – Dennis Roßbach

TABLE OF CONTENTS

CHAPTER ONE

WHAT IS PROCUREMENT?

Because it will provide a thorough knowledge of procurement and supply procedures, it is essential first to understand procurement. The word "procurement" refers to the process or action to source or acquire services or products for a company. Depending on the company, procurement may refer to simply the act of purchasing, or it may include the whole process leading up to the acquisition of goods and services.

Procurement is a term that refers to large-scale purchases made for a company. In the procurement process, there are two parties involved: the buyer and the supplier. However, procurement refers to the act of purchasing rather than the actions of the seller.

When a business utilizes the products or services it procures to create its end product, procurement is part of the input. As a result, it's a critical part of every company's operations. In addition, procuring high-quality products or services at competitive prices is crucial to the buyer's company's success.

Procurement seems to be a straightforward procedure at first glance. While this may be fun, it's frequently very competitive, with considerable attention given to every detail along the way. The following are examples of procurement-related activities:

- ❖ Selecting a Vendor
- ❖ Negotiation of the Amount Owed
- ❖ Vetting in the Long Term
- ❖ Negotiation of a Contract
- ❖ Making the Big Purchase

Direct vs. Indirect Procurement: What's the Difference?

Sourcing the products, resources, or services used as inputs in the company's production process is known as direct procurement. Purchasing immediately affects the company's production of products and services; therefore, it's critical. As a result, the direct buying approach significantly impacts the end product's quality and cost.

If you're using direct procurement, you should know when to use it. Manufacturing firms often use direct buying. Therefore, a strong working connection with the direct suppliers is the goal of the procurement team.

Organizational daily operations need the acquisition of products and services for internal use; a practice is known as indirect procurement. Long-term contracts with suppliers are the most common way to get them.

Software licenses may be procured via IT services procurement. It's called services procurement, and it's a one-time, very short-term deal.

Indirect Sourcing

- ❖ Purchasing Done Through Unusual Means
- ❖ Sourcing of goods and services
- ❖ the acquisition and/or manufacture of products and/or services
- ❖ buying and obtaining products and services for one's usage
- ❖ Management of temporary workers as well as the provision of advisory services
- ❖ Items for selling and raw materials
- ❖ Services such as utility management, facilities management, and travel are examples.

Examples include paying for specialized services, software subscriptions, and so on. Increases revenue and profits from outside the company is in charge of running the business daily to fill up the gaps in processes and people is made up of pre-production materials or components used to make purchases of nonperishables and consumables.

Used to pay for third-party services and hire more employees create long-term, collaborative partnerships with your suppliers. Use transactional, short-term relationships with providers as a last resort maintain contractual agreements with providers that are limited in scope.

What's the procedure for procuring goods and services?

So, what's the procedure for procuring goods and services? Sourcing is defined as the identification and execution by companies of specific procedures to guarantee their ability to purchase products and services to fulfill and accomplish their goals. When it comes to saving money, the procurement process matters since it directly affects it. Continuous evaluation of the procurement process guarantees that the company's objectives are being fulfilled. It may be adjusted when a process isn't functioning as expected or when it runs into difficulties. Businesses must make sure they get the most out of their procurement process to maximize efficiency.

Because each company's requirements differ, the procurement procedure isn't uniform for everyone. Each company has a unique set of criteria, and as a result, its procurement process will vary from the procurement process of another company with different specifications.

Flowchart of the Purchasing Process

The procurement process flow differs from organization to organization. In practice, procurement typically begins with recognizing a need and then drafting a purchase order outlining all of the needs' specifications in detail. When making a purchase, the purchase order will be submitted to the appropriate procurement or finance team for approval if the need currently has an approved supplier. If it's denied, you'll get a rejection letter along with the reason why. The purchase order becomes a buy requisition after it has been approved.

Because there isn't a preapproved supplier or vendor, the procurement team issues numerous RFQs, each with specific details on the order's needs. After evaluating the bids submitted, a suitable vendor is chosen. Finally, an agreement is negotiated with the selected vendor, and a purchase order is sent.

A three-way matching verification is performed on the vendor's invoice once the bought goods are received. A three-way matching is performed by comparing and verifying the purchase order, vendors' invoice, and products received. The purpose of this stage is to see whether the organization did place the order with the designated vendor and if the vendor delivered and billed the goods following the purchase order. If the order was received as requested and as invoiced, this is compared to the receipt of the products.

The vendor's invoice is approved, and payment is issued to the supplier after the three-way verification is complete. The finance department is in charge of accounting for the transaction.

The Procurement Process Has Several Stages. The procurement process is broken down as follows:

- ❖ The Determination of Need
- ❖ Determination of Requirement Specifics
- ❖ Sourcing
- ❖ Price and terms are negotiated and then finalized.
- ❖ Purchase Order and Requisition
- ❖ The Purchase Order Has Arrived.
- ❖ Expediting
- ❖ Providing and Inspecting Products/Services
- ❖ Process of Making a Payment
- ❖ Keeping Records And Conducting Reviews
- ❖ The method of identifying a need

Recognizing a need is the first step in making a purchase. The requirement to purchase a new item or to restock something when it is needed or falls below a particular stock level may be identified in this way. Most companies will need to go through a requisition procedure to get this. This consultation with all stakeholders is critical to avoid problems later in the procurement process.

Establishing the Particulars of the Requirement

If a need is found, the product or service details must be agreed upon before moving further. Technical requirements and component numbers are examples of what might fall under this category. This list of more information is produced with the agreement of all the technical personnel concerned if the item is not already purchased. Preventing costly blunders later in the procurement process requires precise details and appropriate engagement with all departments involved.

Purchasing

Once a particular item or service is decided upon, the procurement team must research to identify the different suppliers that provide it. If you place many orders with the same vendor over and over again, you'll have a list of preferred suppliers. Vendor identification and vetting take more time for a new product. Working with a pre-existing vendor who is already known to be a reliable provider saves time. Identifying new suppliers will require a comprehensive investigation into their track record, timeliness, quality, dependability, and pricing.

During this period, companies like Beroe can assist procurement departments by providing the market intelligence data they need to make well-informed choices.

Once the procurement department has researched suppliers and requested bids for the required goods, it's time to choose a supplier. This is a critical step since before making a final choice, factors including reputation, pricing, speed of service, and reliability must be considered. Three quotations are the standard, but your company will need to decide the best practice for this rule of thumb. Management approval will be required depending on the sourcing choices and associated expenses. The request for proposals, bids, or tenders will have to be publicized if the order is subject to a bidding or tendering procedure.

Price and terms negotiations and finalization

Requests for quotations will be made to the selected suppliers for direct purchasing. Before making a decision, it's customary to get at least three quotations. The quote's competitiveness in terms of price and turnaround time will be evaluated. While choosing a supplier, consider not just pricing but also promptness, dependability, and quality when making your decision.

Depending on the terms and circumstances of the purchase, the qualified offers will be selected via a bidding or tendering procedure.

Following the established procedure, the chosen provider will be picked and publicized transparently. The selection of bids should be fair and transparent to guarantee that buyers receive the greatest value for their money and supply quality. When the selection process is harmed, the value of the products or services provided may also be affected.

Having a single high-volume supplier vs. selecting numerous providers is now up to the customer. The more significant number of orders you have with a single supplier offers you more negotiating leverage when it comes to pricing.

A single supplier, on the other hand, not being able to meet an order has an impact on the whole production process. One may negotiate lower prices by using more than one supplier for a given item. However, this limits the amount of opportunity for negotiation. Having a large number of vendors on hand may assist in creating price and quality competition.

Order And Purchase Request

Appropriate authority will authorize an internal purchase order request. As a result, a purchase order will be generated that includes all of the transaction details, including terms and conditions. Some businesses engage the customer in creating the order's details so that both parties are aware of them. For the sake of accuracy, the specifications must be thoroughly compared to the purchase order and the quotation from the supplier.

The Purchase Order Is Delivered

The buyer is notified once a shipment has been made. The buyer and seller's procedures determine how the purchase order is delivered. Alternatively, you may fax or email your request. Both the buyer and the seller agreed on these details, so everything fits together nicely.

Expedited Delivery

A timetable for timely delivery of requested products or services must be created, accounting for any unexpected delays. Payment and delivery details may also be included.

Supply and inspection of goods and services

The buyer receives the finished product or service when it is ready. The buyer is in charge of making sure the delivered goods comply with the purchase order. The buyer has the option of accepting it or rejecting it. Both choices will set in motion events following the terms and circumstances that have been agreed upon. As soon as the customer accepts delivery of the goods, the payment procedure begins.

Process of Making a Payment

The papers associated with the order must be examined to process the payment. The original purchase order, the goods received, and the payment request invoice is all compared to ensure everything is correct. Before payment is made, any discrepancies are corrected. Once the payment has been authorized, the funds are sent following the payment methods that were previously agreed upon.

Maintaining And Reviewing Records

Companies, buyers, and sellers must all keep detailed records for audit and taxation purposes to conduct audits and taxation. The whole process should be reviewed regularly to ensure it's working correctly and resolve any disagreements that may emerge. Reevaluation improves procurement efficiency while also reducing the likelihood of future conflicts.

The procurement process outlined above differs from company to company, but the logical flow is the same across. Procurement efficiency ensures timely delivery of bought products and services.

All parties must keep up with discussions at all relevant stages of the process to guarantee that the products and services purchased are precisely what is needed, up to the highest standards, and priced competitively. Excellent record-keeping is beneficial not only for checking the records but also for restocking the same products. An adequate supply of high-quality goods is ensured by careful vendor selection.

Purchasing Components

Procurement has three main parts:

Those involved

Procurement staffing levels are determined by how much manufacturing and procurement work is sold. Procurement employees are few and far between in a small business. A whole staff manages the buying process for the bigger companies. The number of approvals is also lower when ordering low-value goods. A greater degree of approval is required in management for purchase requisitions involving large or significant purchases.

Steps in the Procedure

To work effectively, the procurement process must be properly thought out and structured. Inefficient and inconsistent procurement departments may create delays and issues with purchases and payments, contributing to the weak and unstable process. In addition, it's essential to keep the process transparent to avoid corruption or manipulation.

Records or Documentation

Keep meticulous records at all times throughout the procurement process. Even though nearly all stages in the process are digital, it is critical for both the buyer and the seller that all essential information be recorded efficiently at each level and coordinated and compared at each stage.

Acquiring, Purchasing and the Supply Chain: A Comprehensive Overview

Procurement, purchasing, and supply chain are words that are often used interchangeably by businesses. The supply chain, on the other hand, is the most complex. The procurement process is only one link in the chain of supplies. Procurement is a stage in the purchasing process.

Purchasing vs. Procurement: In what way does the purchasing procedure work?

An organization's needs may be identified, the requirements obtained, and an effective working relationship with suppliers maintained via the procurement process. Procurement research finds potential providers after a requirement has been established.

The purchasing procedure, on the other hand, is a sub-function. It involves getting the purchase order, assessing the RFQs, creating a buy order, receiving the requested goods/services, confirming their quality, and then processing the payment. That's all.

Even while procurement and buying have some overlap, many individuals mistakenly consider them to be the same thing. This is not the case because their objectives, definitions, methods, and areas of emphasis are wholly distinct. Compare and contrast how procurement and buying vary.

Aspects of procurement include selecting, identifying, and purchasing products and services from vendors via a variety of procedures, as well as negotiating with them. Direct purchase and tendering are examples of acquisition procedures. Procurement requires that the products and services be supplied on time or earlier, as stated in the PO, as well as that the correct quantity of goods and services is provided to the company. While procurement focuses on obtaining products and services that a company needs, buying doesn't. The word "procurement" covers more than just the act of making purchases. In other words, procurement includes buying.

Both of these procedures have different stages involved. Before making a purchase request, you must first establish the business need. After that, you must authorize the request, approve it, and then look for potential suppliers. The next step is to make inquiries, find out the supplier's quotes, and then negotiate. Additionally, procurement entails carefully choosing the supplier and then receiving the products to verify they are of the required quality and keeping invoices for future reference after three-way matching.

The last step of procurement entails paying the vendor. Buying is a lot easier now since there are fewer stages to complete. PO acknowledgment, receiving and checking products, keeping invoices, verifying the invoice's validity, and paying the supplier are all stages in the process.

Procurement is seen as strategic, whereas buying is viewed as tactical when it comes to business functions. This is because procurement begins as soon as the company identifies a need and concludes after the supplier has been paid for items delivered. It includes actions such as assessing several suppliers before placing an order with one of them. Additionally, it includes making sure that the contracts formed have the greatest possible value. Instead of focusing on the acquisition of products and services, purchasing consists only of transactional activities. It doesn't have the same complexity as procurement, yet it nevertheless performs the same job.

The procurement function is necessary for a company's requirements to be met. Finding a need is only the beginning; making sure that need is met most effectively. These requirements are met since it considers the whole picture from beginning to end. The proactive approach to procurement means that issues are prevented before they ever arise, which may be described as such. Purchasing is distinct from other types of spending since it's more of a response. When a need arises, it fulfills the needs of the company. You might say that it's all about getting things done to commit money to a company when it comes to buying.

Preventing supply chain and business function issues starts with assessing procurement's risk assessment. By reducing the risk, possible problems may be addressed before they worsen. When procuring, for example, the risks associated with different suppliers are carefully weighed and evaluated. Procurement also entails evaluating various risks, including data security risks and operational risks. However, unlike procurement, purchasing does not place as much emphasis on reducing or eliminating risk as does procurement. Thus the two are distinct—a transactional approach to purchasing means that risk assessment and mitigation aren't a priority.

Each function has distinct objectives, and as a consequence, the things they achieve vary. For example, procurement aims to generate value and consider the total cost of ownership throughout the process of purchasing. On the other hand, purchasing is a more fundamental activity since it focuses on the order's cost and how to obtain the greatest deal. Procurement is ongoing because the individuals involved in it are concerned about maintaining appropriate supplier relationships and continuously evaluating other procedures. However, unlike procurement, once products and services are purchased, the procurement process ends.

Purchasing doesn't pay attention to supplier connections, while procurement does. On the other hand, procurement is concerned with the long term, while buying is more concerned with the immediate future. To guarantee long-term savings and advantages, it's critical for businesses to maintain good relationships with their suppliers. Procurement stresses finding the finest suppliers who can fulfill those needs and maintain those relationships after being established.

The buying department works with the company's existing supplier network. To make sure they're working with the appropriate vendors that provide high-quality services and on-time deliveries, procurement goes further.

The difference between sourcing and procuring

In the procurement process, a requirement is identified, a supplier is found, an order is placed, delivery is received, a payment is made, and the transaction is documented. Inventory and storage are included since it is necessary to determine the requirement for a specific item. Much work is involved in ensuring the buyer receives the best bargain possible, including negotiating and preparation.

Additionally, relationship management should be part of procurement so that suppliers can retain quality supply while also offering preferred prices and conditions. You'll have to follow up to ensure everything goes well and according to plan during the procurement process.

The buyer verifies whether the material meets the need once it is delivered and received before accepting it and releasing payment. Procurement includes the whole record-keeping process, from the requisition request all the way through to the release of the money.

Procurement is also the initial step in the whole supply chain since the company often utilizes the purchased goods to produce the products that they then sell to others. Lack of procurement or delays may bring down the whole business. It is an essential procedure for any manufacturing firm. The quality of the company's production process will suffer if the products it purchases do not meet the required specifications or are of low quality. Any anomalies in the procurement process significantly impact the quality and timeliness of any product a business produces.

While sourcing is an essential part of the procurement process, it is just one stage. A company's study into possible sources of what they need to purchase is called sourcing. This is done by consulting with specialists and reading market data. Ordering from a verified source is easy if the goods being purchased are repeat orders. The buyer should, however, constantly be aware of any new competitors entering the market. When a buyer is aware of market dynamics, they can take advantage of such developments.

If the procurement process is interrupted due to unexpected events, a company should not become too dependent on a single supplier. Having more than one supplier is always a good idea to guarantee that a pre-approved provider is always available. It's also more challenging to negotiate low prices when there's just one supplier.

It takes considerably longer to source a brand-new item for the customer. To begin with, it must be established whether the desired item is available from a supplier. Identifying companies that accept bespoke orders is necessary if no current suppliers are available for the specific item. A comprehensive investigation and verification of the item's likely origins are required once they have been discovered. Shortlisted companies must be contacted with details about the need once they have been identified.

Negotiating the price at which the item will be delivered without sacrificing quality is the next critical stage in sourcing. Purchases made with little consideration for quality will result in defective finished goods since people tend to go for the lowest options accessible. Procurement costs may cut into a buyer's profit margin if they're too high. An overpriced procurement will raise the price of final produced products, making them less competitive in the market.

Sourcing must strike a delicate balance between obtaining high-quality products while also keeping costs reasonable. An organization's profit margins benefit from every dollar saved when purchasing raw materials. However, quality raw materials are also critical to a manufacturing company's ability to maintain its high standards.

Another essential consideration when selecting a raw material supplier is the source's reliability. Delays caused by the supplier may cause the whole production process to be delayed or even stopped. Even if they charge a bit more, providers are often preferred because of their dependability and speed of delivery. It's worth it to spend a little more to minimize risk when sourcing a critical component.

The difference between procurement and supply chain management

Procurement is the process that begins with determining that an item is needed and continues through the steps of ordering, receiving, and paying for it. Only the acquisition and payment of the received goods are covered. To begin the supply chain, the first step is to acquire the required goods or services.

However, it includes all steps from obtaining raw materials to manufacturing and supplying completed products to delivering them to the ultimate user. An item goes through the whole manufacturing and distribution process in the supply chain, from raw materials to finished goods.

- ❖ Supply chain stages are as follows: there are
- ❖ Sources for the primary material
- ❖ The manufacturing process is divided into many phases.
- ❖ Getting to and from wholesalers
- ❖ Warehousing
- ❖ delivering the merchandise to retail outlets, and
- ❖ Purchase by the general public

Quality control and logistics are present at every step. As a result, procurement is just one stage in the lengthy supply chain process.

A Guide to Purchasing

One of the most critical stages in the supply chain of any product is procurement. This activity has an impact on a company's profit margins and the quality of its raw materials. The five procurement principles should be kept in mind at all times by any procurement department. When a business follows these five procurement pillars, it will have the most efficient and cost-effective procurement process available.

Procurement's five pillars promote free and fair commerce, which helps the economy develop. Vendors have an equal opportunity to be awarded business based on their merits when used on a smaller scale.

The Five Procurement Pillars

1. Value

There are times when the most expensive choice is the better one for suppliers. The value should be the driving force behind the procurement process. The customer needs to obtain the greatest deal on a quality product. When a customer sacrifices input quality to save money, it harms the final product or service of the business. The best way to choose a supplier is to prioritize value for money above all other considerations.

2. Unrestricted Rivalry

They are creating a transparent and bias-free vendor selection process guarantees that all vendors are on equal footing. The buyer who can get the most bang for his buck will profit from this free-market competition.

3. Transparency and ethical conduct

Corruption is highly likely to occur throughout the vendor selection process, whether it's done via direct purchase, a tender, or a bid. The quality and value of the goods bought will be compromised if unethical tactics are used to influence the vendor selection process.

4. Taking Responsibility and Keeping Records

Everyone involved in the procurement process should be held responsible for their decisions and actions. In addition, having reasonable record-keeping procedures makes it simpler to follow the procurement process from start to finish.

5. Equity

All players have an equal opportunity to thrive when a fair and consistent procurement procedure is ensured across sectors.

Models for Purchasing

A procurement model is a set of procedures used by a company or organization when procuring goods or services. Models of procurement also describe the levels of procurement hierarchy, control, and decision-making.

The specifics of a procurement strategy vary from firm to company, depending on their industry and business climate.

Many departments and divisions may or may not be geographically dispersed in big corporations. Management decisions may be made either centrally or locally. Based on who controls the purchase process, procurement models may be categorized.

Procurement Model at the Local Level

The control and decision-making are decentralized in this procurement approach since they are made locally or departmentally. It would be up to the local department or division to complete all procurement choices. This approach is based on the idea that local management knows the department's requirements better than anyone else. It allows for more agility in the procurement process, as well as a reduction in administrative layers. Maverick spending choices without considering the big picture are always a possibility.

Model for Centralized Purchasing

When using the centralized procurement approach, central management has complete authority over all purchase choices. All procurement is subject to a centralized approval procedure, and the effective regulations also apply to all local decisions. With this procurement approach, purchasing choices are made while keeping in mind the company's or organization's total budget and expenditures. Personnel with expertise and dedication negotiate the purchases. Bulk buying has the added benefit of lower costs. However, there's a chance you won't satisfy all of the specific criteria for your area. Many levels of bureaucracy complicate the procedure.

A model with a Blended Engine

A hybrid procurement approach combines localized and centralized procurement in certain companies. Other purchases are centralized, and some are local under this approach. With this approach, all local departments have a degree of autonomy within the administrative control while benefiting from both models. The center-led method of procurement is another name for it.

Categories Of Sourcing

Indirect Sourcing

A company may buy the inputs it needs to make its finished product directly from the supplier. This is what a manufacturing-related company needs when it comes to raw materials. Direct procurement's input costs and efficiency are critical to a company's profitability and success. A snag in direct procurement compromises the company's capacity to produce its goods.

Purchasing Done Through Unusual Means

When services or input are purchased that aren't utilized directly in the production of a company's product but are necessary for day-to-day operations, indirect procurement occurs. For example, it could contain office supplies or equipment maintenance services. Indirect procurement can harm the company's operations.

Life Cycle of Procurement

The procurement life cycle stages of a business are typically customized to meet the specific requirements of that organization. Depending on the company, the procurement life cycle stages may be consolidated or broken out further.

Analyzing Needs and Creating a Persona

Identifying the need and details of what needs to be purchased is the first step in the procurement process. Next, actual business requirements, budget allocations, and other data should be gathered inside the organization. External market research is then conducted, and information on the item's cost and further basic details are obtained. Data collected both internally and outside at this stage forms the foundation for the procurement plan that will be executed in its entirety later. At this point in the procurement life cycle, individuals from all levels of the organization are involved and information from outside the company.

Strategic Purchasing and Sourcing Plan

A sourcing strategy is developed based on the information gathered during the initial stage of the procurement process. If a policy has already been implemented, it may be tweaked to meet current needs better and remove inefficiencies that arose in the past.

Identify Potential Suppliers and Build a Supplier Portfolio

An initial market study's data may be processed to provide a list of supplier criteria. The pre-approved supplier portfolio is a list of vendors selected following discussions with them that certain companies use. To obtain better prices and value, the business benefits from having a pre-approved supplier list to work together to develop that connection. In addition, it saves time by eliminating the need to negotiate with new potential vendors each time a procurement need arises

The Request for Proposal (RFP) and the Process of Making

Using an RFP template and criteria from the procurement, a new RFP may be generated or an old one updated. The guidelines governing the selecting procedure have been laid forth.

Selection And Negotiation Processes

Choosing a vendor and negotiating the best price and conditions for the purchase are key steps in the procurement process.

Integrate and improve the supplier's performance

An organization's supplier is incorporated into the entire process after the sourcing procedure for new suppliers is put in place. Any problems will be dealt with, and the supply will be fine-tuned to provide the best efficiency and value possible.

Analyze And Compare

Once it is complete, an evaluation of the procurement life cycle should take place to ensure everything is running well. The procurement process with the supplier should have particular standouts in terms of performance or failure. In the future procurement lifecycle, these lessons should be put into practice. Being receptive to the supplier's and other stakeholders' comments may assist in determining whether or not there is room for improvement.

Planned Purchases

Customer satisfaction is not only based on whether or not the product meets the customer's expectations. The ability to fulfill demand on schedule while maintaining quality is equally critical. To prepare for potential changes in demand, companies use a technique known as demand planning. Knowledge of all variables that may influence demand must be present to achieve this.

When demand planning goes wrong, there are two outcomes: a shortage of products to satisfy demand or an overstocked inventory that is sitting on the shelf unclaimed. Both possibilities have an economic effect on the business. Demand planning aids the business in anticipating and responding to changes in demand to maximize revenue and satisfy customers.

Forecasting

Organizations benefit greatly from proactive demand planning as opposed to reactive demand management. The most efficient use of money and other resources occurs when a company correctly anticipates demand fluctuations and appropriately changes the procurement and supply chain.

It's just as essential to know the present market climate and variables that may affect demand as it is to have historical demand data. Current events, natural disasters, and other political problems are examples of these influences. Accurate demand planning requires comprehensive data collection and analysis. It is becoming more and more automatic as technology progresses.

Why Demand Planning Is A Good Idea

Proper management of the supply chain

A company may better predict demand surges using demand planning. As a result, its supply network is capable of supporting a more lavish production rate as needed. During times of intense demand, every step of the supply chain is meticulously planned out in advance.

The whole process is more likely to go well if all players, from procurement suppliers through the manufacturing line, are ready. The more customers know in advance, the fewer complaints there will be if there are delays because of demand surges. Getting everyone engaged in the negotiation process early on will result in more favorable terms and more transparency. Maintenance and servicing operations may be better planned based on demand forecasts if necessary.

Production and labor management that is up to standard

By anticipating demand fluctuations, you can guarantee that you have the right amount of employees on hand at all times. It's a waste of money to hire too many people when demand is declining. When demand spikes, having too few workers on hand may cause production to go off the rails. It's easier to budget for more outstanding production when demand is planned ahead of time. Managing capacity, resources, and production efficiency all improve when all elements of production meet demand.

Proper Control of Cash Flows

A company may better manage its cash flow by predicting the demand pattern. Unsold inventory or raw materials don't get locked up as cash. Financial planners may arrange for extra loans to cover a deficit if they anticipate a decline in demand.

Supply Chain Management Models

When an organization or company wants to buy goods or services, it will use a procurement model. Procurement models also specify the hierarchy, control, and decision-making processes involved in the process. Many procurement model specifics are determined by the business context in which a firm operates.

Many departments and divisions exist in big organizations, some of which may or may not be geographically dispersed. Centralized decision-making or decentralized decision-making are both possible. Models of procurement may be categorized according to who has authority over the purchase process.

Procurement Model at the Local Level

Control and decision-making are decentralized in this procurement approach since it does not use a central clearinghouse. It would be up to the department or division in question to make all of the purchasing choices. Because local management is more in tune with the department's specific requirements, this approach makes sense. It streamlines the procurement process and makes it more responsive to customer needs. Whenever you make unwise financial choices without considering the big picture, you run the danger of blowing your budget.

Procurement Model with Centralized Management:

Central management has complete control over purchase choices when using a centralized procurement approach. Procurement choices are made at the local level following the central approval procedure, which the whole organization follows. This procurement model's goal is to keep in mind the company's total budget and expenditures while making purchases. Personnel with expertise and dedication negotiate the purchases. Bulk buying also offers a lower cost-benefit. However, there's a chance you won't satisfy all of the specific criteria for your area. In addition, the procedure is slowed down by a thicket of red tape.

A model with a Mixture of Electric and Gasoline Power:

Using a hybrid style of procurement, which combines localized and centralized procurement, is an option for certain companies. Other purchases are centralized, and some are local under this approach. This approach combines both models' best features while allowing local departments some degree of autonomy under the overall organizational control. The center-led approach of procurement is another name for it.

Different Forms Of Procurement

Indirect Sourcing

A company may buy the inputs it needs to make its finished product directly from the supplier. This is what a manufacturing-related company typically needs in terms of raw material. An essential element in determining a company's profitability and success is how much it costs and how efficient it is. An impediment to the company's capacity to produce its goods occurs when direct procurement is delayed.

Purchasing Done Through Other Means (Indirect Procurement)

Purchase of services or input that is not directly utilized in the production of a company's product but is necessary for daily operations is referred to as indirect procurement. Office supplies and equipment maintenance services are examples of what could be included. Interrupts in the supply chain may harm the company.

Cycle of Purchasing

Each stage of the procurement life cycle is specifically designed to meet the requirements of the business involved. As a result, some businesses' procurement life cycle stages may be consolidated, while others may have further sub-categorization.

Category of Needs Analysis and Personality Profiling

The business must first define the demand and the details of what needs to be purchased in this procurement stage. Next, actual business requirements, budget allocations, and other data should be gathered inside the organization. After that, the business will do market research on the outside to learn more about the item's price and other basic characteristics. Data collected both internally and outside at this stage forms the foundation for the procurement plan that will be executed in its entirety later on. At this point in the procurement life cycle, individuals from all levels of the organization are involved and information from outside the company.

The Strategy for Procurement and Sourcing

After gathering data in the first stage of the procurement process, companies develop a sourcing strategy based on that information. Adapting an existing policy to meet current needs and remove issues and inefficiencies may be done if one already exists.

Perform Supplier Evaluation & Build Supplier Portfolios

Data from the first market research may be used to develop a supplier selection criteria list. Then, supplier portfolios, which include a pre-approved list of suppliers that have been selected following discussions, are operated by certain companies. To obtain better prices and value, the business benefits from having a pre-approved list of suppliers. It also saves the time usually spent negotiating with new potential suppliers whenever a procurement need arises.

Request for Proposal (RFP) and Selection

An RFP template and criteria may be developed from scratch or adapted from an existing RFP for the procurement. This process's guidelines are laid forth.

The process of negotiating and selecting

The procurement process culminates when a vendor is chosen and agreed upon the best price and conditions.

Integrate and improve the supplier's performance

An organization's supplier is incorporated into the entire process after the sourcing procedure for new suppliers is put in place. Therefore, no problems will be dealt with and adjusted to maximize efficiency and value.

Conduct a Review and Set a Goal

Once it's completed, it's essential to watch the procurement life cycle to ensure everything runs well. In addition, it's necessary to keep an eye out for anything that stands out in the buying process with the supplier. All of these lessons should be put into practice in the next round of procurements. Being receptive to supplier and other stakeholders' input may assist in finding potential areas for development.

Supply Chain Management

Consumer happiness is not only dependent on the product fulfilling the expectations of the customer. It's also a matter of being able to fulfill demand while maintaining high quality. An organization's ability to correctly anticipate and prepare for future demand variations is called demand planning. To do this, it is necessary to be aware of all the variables that may influence demand.

Either there will be defective products to satisfy demand when demand planning fails, or there will be too many goods on hand, all of which remain unsold. Both possibilities have an economic effect on the business. Demand planning aids the business in anticipating and responding to changes in demand to maximize revenue and satisfy customers.

Forecasting

An organization's demand planning is most effective when it is proactive rather than reactive in response to changing demand. With precise demand forecasting and supply chain adjustments, a company can most use its money and other resources.

Knowing the present market situation and variables that may affect it is necessary for accurately forecasting future demand. Current events, natural disasters, and other political problems are examples of these influences. Data collection and analysis are essential for precise demand planning. Currently, this procedure is being mechanized in response to advancements in technology.

Planning For Demand Has Many Benefits

Management Of Supply Chains In A Proper Manner

Using demand planning, a business may better anticipate demand surges. It guarantees that their supply network can support a tremendous production pace. All supply chain stages are planned to ensure seamless operations during times of high demand. The whole process is more likely to go well if all players, from procurement suppliers through the manufacturing line, are ready. If demand surges are likely to cause delays, providing customers with a prior warning will result in fewer complaints. Better conditions and more openness may be negotiated in advance with all parties concerned. Maintenance and servicing operations may be better planned based on demand forecasts if necessary.

Proper Management Of Production And Labor

By anticipating demand peaks and troughs, you'll have the perfect amount of employees on hand. Spending money on too many employees when demand is declining is a waste. A shortage of workers during a high-demand period may cause the manufacturing line to go off course. It's easier to budget for temporary workers when demand planning is used to control increasing output. Capacity management, resource management, and production efficiency simultaneously improve when all production elements sync with customer demand.

Managing Cash Flows Correctly

A company may better manage its cash flow by predicting the demand pattern. Unsold inventory or raw materials don't get locked up as cash. Financial planners may arrange for extra loans to cover a deficit if they anticipate a decline in demand.

CHAPTER TWO

WHAT NEXT?
THE FUTURE OF PROCUREMENT

The procurement process is constantly changing to keep up with the market's shifting demands. In addition, procurement management is always evolving as organizations and companies expand beyond national boundaries.

The use of eProcurement technologies and software has lowered procurement cycle costs while improving efficiency. These systems' user interfaces, or UIs, are growing more pleasant to end-users every day. Due to the installation of procurement management applications, real-time data is now flowing seamlessly across all levels of management. Thanks to the digitalization of procurement, best practices and openness have never been simpler to implement than they are now. Data analysis, demand forecasting, and procurement management have become more of a science than a risk thanks to machine learning, Big Data, and AI. In addition, the eProcurement system is now more readily available thanks to cloud-based technologies.

When the Covid-19 or new Coronavirus/Coronavirus epidemic in China halted supply chains, it clearly showed the global aspect of procurement. Lockdowns were implemented by nations across the world, putting the whole globe into a state of emergency. Companies with a broad network of suppliers from various regions were better equipped to utilize alternative suppliers rapidly. Because of this crisis, it's become apparent how critical it is to develop and execute effective supplier risk management strategies.

More agile and responsive procurement processes can better deal with the aftermath of such catastrophes and reduce the financial and human toll. Emergency sourcing choices are now more straightforward to make and execute because of procurement's digital revolution.

The Rubik's Cube solver determines how many rotations are necessary to complete the puzzle.

What is procurement's use of artificial intelligence (AI)?

The Evolution of Artificial Intelligence

We have to go back to the beginning to comprehend where we are today. Contrary to popular belief, artificial intelligence has been around since the 10th century BC, when the term "artificial" was first used.

1951 saw the first mention of a computer program with artificial intelligence capabilities comparable to those of today's systems. Christopher Strachey and Dietrich Prinz developed chess and checkers software for the University of Manchester's Ferranti Mark 1 computer with Dietrich Prinz. It was a game-changer, even if it wasn't as advanced as the technology available today.

Today's Artificial Intelligence

Today, when we think of AI-based applications, we generally picture Amazon's Alexa or Apple's Siri. AI, on the other hand, goes well beyond simple virtual assistants. In virtually every area of our everyday life, artificial intelligence (AI) is utilized widely; AI is used and driven in almost everything we use. Modern technology is capable of changing its behavior and picking up on new concepts and procedures. As a result, it's a gold mine for businesses of all sizes because it can connect disparate systems and technology and make complex problems easier to see.

Here are some current applications of artificial intelligence (AI):

- ❖ Robotics manufacturing
- ❖ Autonomous vehicles
- ❖ Agents that know how to arrange trips well
- ❖ Personal assistants who work with you virtually
- ❖ Mapping out the various ailments
- ❖ Automated investment in the financial markets
- ❖ Chatbots that engage in conversation with the user
- ❖ Tools for Natural Language Processing
- ❖ Types of artificial intelligence (AI)

If you don't know what you're searching for, it may be tough to sort among the many kinds of AI. An easy method to tell which artificial intelligence program is better is to look at what it can accomplish. AI may be divided into four broad categories:

Machines That React Quickly

This kind of artificial intelligence is straightforward and is set up to provide predictable results depending on the data that it gets as input. All artificial intelligence in this category will act in the same manner no matter what the situation is. It's unable to change its behavior or understand emotional factors. Netflix's movie suggestion engine is an excellent example of this.

Memory Capacity Issues

A tiny amount of memory Artificial intelligence (AI) is capable of learning from the actions and data it has previously gathered. As a result, it is typical for artificial intelligence (AI) to make predictions or execute complicated tasks based on historical data and pre-programmed knowledge.

Mind-Body Theory

We're getting closer and closer to having this kind of AI. This kind of artificial intelligence (AI) is designed to imitate human decision-making processes. While interacting with humans, it can usually analyze, comprehend and recall emotions, which it may subsequently use to alter its behavior.

This kind of intellect, on the other hand, is difficult to duplicate. We've just begun to scratch the surface of what these new technologies are capable of. AI self-driving vehicles are an excellent illustration of the theory of mind.

Being aware of one's own existence

In this kind of AI, the software is aware of its own feelings and those of others. This is the most sophisticated type of AI. It replicates human intellect, wants, and aspirations since it requires a certain degree of awareness. Unfortunately, this self-aware technology cannot be supported at this time due to a lack of adequate infrastructure.

AI that is broad vs. AI that is focused

Strong or restricted AI is a subset of the four types of AI. For example, in films like Terminator, we encounter self-aware or a theory of mind AI that acts and thinks like a human being. The strong AI category includes this kind of artificial intelligence (AI for short).

Contrary to popular belief, the vast majority of artificial intelligence (AI) used in procurement falls into a limited or weak category. Rather than automating routine activities, this kind of AI digs deeper to discover creative solutions to operational challenges.

Definitions of Artificial Intelligence in the Procurement Process

With all the talk about artificial intelligence and associated technologies, it's easy to get lost in the shuffle. You must know what something means to comprehend it fully.

Self-learning or smart algorithm software solutions that replace human procedures are referred to as artificial intelligence (AI) in procurement. Furthermore, AI can interpret complicated systems and resolve problems by utilizing computer software rather than just simplifying remedial chores. All the hard work and leverage may be put into an algorithm that handles contract administration, procurement support, strategic sourcing, and expenditure analysis.

To make use of the vast quantities of data analytics that are now available to procurement experts, AI is accelerating the process. This is something that no other human being can readily duplicate.

Let's start by going through some of the most common AI procurement phrases you'll see:

Artificial intelligence (AI) is called software, and algorithms deemed "smart" and capable of learning new tasks are called artificial intelligence (AI).

Machine Learning (ML): is a collection of algorithms that identify patterns in previous behavior and use them to aid in decision-making or predictions.

An algorithm that can analyze, interpret, and comprehend human language is known as *Natural Language Processing* (NLP).

It is possible to program a robot to do repeated activities by using *robotic process automation* (RPA) software. However, this kind of software AI is not considered by the majority of specialists.

Procurement-specific AI types

Purchasing with a Mindset

Purchasing cognitively is a new word for technology that can imitate human behavior by learning on its own. It's designed to make procurement management easier by handling vast amounts of data. AI processes like these are included.

❖ Observation of Patterns

❖ Computer-Assisted Language Learning (CALL)

❖ Learning from a machine

❖ Extraction of Automated Data

❖ Cognitive Procurement: Challenges and Opportunities

Because it is a novel idea in procurement, there isn't a clear description of what this kind of technology might look like for procurement. However, many artificial intelligence (AI) companies claim that their software resembles human intellect, generating much interest. As a result, it's the answer to all your sourcing problems. Due to the lack of solid proof that such a technology exists for use in procurement.

Robotic Process Automation vs. Artificial Intelligence

These two words are often used interchangeably, which leads to a lot of muddles. For example, despite the fact that RPA has the potential to improve procurement efficiency significantly, it is not necessarily deemed artificial intelligence. In other words, what's the distinction?

For the sake of simplicity, consider AI to be a catch-all phrase that encompasses a wide range of concepts, including robotic process automation (RPA). AI may also be categorized based on how well it can mimic human intellect.

Human-like physical activity is imitated by Robotic Process Automation (RPA). That it can do a physical job again and over again is what distinguishes it from others.

Using AI to Analyze and Classify Spend

AI encompasses both AI-based techniques and ML. RPA has nothing on it. Many of the AI-based procurement apps we see today are ML-based. Machine learning is a branch of artificial intelligence that can learn from experience and apply that knowledge to new situations. However, depending on its purpose, it still needs human supervision and input.

There are many kinds of artificial intelligence (AI) that utilize machine learning throughout the procurement. These are the names of them:

In supervised learning ML, data and patterns from the past are used as input. Then, humans guide the machine by giving the correct answers, which it uses to learn. This kind of AI may be seen, for example, in the categorization of spending.

New and distinctive patterns may be discovered by using an unsupervised learning method. It operates independently and isn't concerned about doing things right. Instead, the emphasis is on finding meaningful patterns in the data. This artificial intelligence will be of no help in the procurement process.

Reward learning is a subset of ML that is more theoretical in nature. Here, the AI's objective is to determine how to act in various situations autonomously. The AI is awarded or penalized based on its choices. That's how it collects data on what to do and how to do it, in that order. Artificial intelligence (AI) is intended to think and operate like a human brain. Deep learning is the most recommended form of machine learning (ML).

What Spend Classification Presents Us With

Classification and expenditure analysis has long been a problem for many in the business, even before AI arrived.

When companies attempt to combine AI and expenditure categorization, there seems to be a significant issue, even though AI is praised for its capacity to improve efficiency. One of the main reasons for this problem is that the AI is designed to automatically classify millions of transactions based on huge amounts of data from invoices, buy orders, and so on into usable procurement categories.

In other cases, companies have devised elaborate ranking systems for categorizing expenditure to circumvent the issue. This has been a challenge because of the sheer amount of data accessible, which comes from a variety of sources. Quality data entry has also proven problematic for businesses to maintain consistency. Because so many companies now need precise real-time data, traditional procurement expenditure analyses were done only annually or quarterly.

Artificial Intelligence for Procurement in Natural Language

Applied natural language processing (NLP) aims to interpret and comprehend human language. This kind of artificial intelligence (AI) technology may offer insights from data or new procedures that aid procurement efficiency. Here are a few typical procurement examples to get you started:

Management of contracts

Procurement contracts are crucial because they include critical information. Unfortunately, procurement experts have always had difficulty accessing this data since it was only available via a variety of sources.

Text parsing algorithms now have access to this important information because of advances in natural language processing (NLP). Artificial intelligence (AI) can scan and analyze large contracts, extracting valuable information. Optical character recognition software, for example, can go one step further using AI. This artificial intelligence makes use of natural language processing (NLP) to recognize text in pictures or physical copies of contracts.

Embedding of text

Word embedding is a great use of NLP in procurement. To bridge the gap between human and machine language, AI can map words and convert them into machine language, which is often composed of numbers. With the use of word embedding, the AI can better categorize and evaluate purchase order texts and identify purchases that fall under a specific category.

Automated Natural Language Processing for Conversational Agents

As far as NLP applications go, this is perhaps the most well-known. Because of NLP usage, voice and virtual assistants like Alexa and Siri can follow human language input.

So, where does artificial intelligence (AI) fit in procurement?

Many procedures in the procurement industry were done manually in the past. However, AI-based solutions may also decode complicated systems and resolve problems by utilizing computer software and simplifying these remedial activities. In addition, many tasks can be automated using an algorithm that performs all the hard lifting and provides you with the actionable information you need.

AI also aids procurement workers in managing their data and getting insight into vast quantities of data more quickly. But, again, this is something that no other human being can readily duplicate.

Why is it necessary for procurement departments to use artificial intelligence (AI)?

Even in procurement, data is a significant asset in today's environment. Procurement teams will have a difficult time tracking expenditure and managing relationships with suppliers and vendors if they lack adequate data. However, it is possible to manage expenses and identify supplier or vendor performance risks by collecting more accurate data.

A scarcity mindset is common among procurement teams when making buying choices. You can provide excellent products and services to your consumers at a price they'll enjoy if you make sure your choices are based on facts you can trust. It offers you a leg up on your rivals in the market.

Artificial intelligence is an excellent match for procurement because, as previously stated, it may offer information that helps make decisions. But you're still not convinced? Others in the procurement sector, on the other hand, have recognized the advantages of using AI in procurement.

A Deloitte study conducted in 2019 found that 51% of CPOs utilize sophisticated analytics. Twenty-five percent of those surveyed said they had tested an artificial intelligence (AI) or cognitive solution in their procurement efforts. Compared to last year, this represents an increase of 19 percent.

What are the uses of artificial intelligence (AI) in sourcing and procurement?

In-depth knowledge of how artificial intelligence works in the procurement process is a huge asset. This expertise is critical, particularly in light of the rapid advancements in technology.

It may take some time to figure out how to use AI in your buying procedures. After all, it's a piece of software, and it should function as efficiently as possible across all departments. Consequently, we have created the following roadmap for how AI is now being used.

Using artificial intelligence in the procurement process is one example.

AI in procurement is still a young field. However, there are several instances where it has already been used. The following are examples of typical applications you may run into:

e-Strategic Sourcing will benefit from data analysis.

Using natural language processing (NLP), strategic sourcing may use AI to collect crucial data like supplier lists using natural language processing (NLP). Data and spending analysis, along with artificial intelligence, have revolutionized procurement sourcing.

AI can streamline sourcing as one of its primary roles. As a result, companies may discover problems with sourcing, such as:

- ❖ Terms of payment that are either expensive or too complicated to compete with
- ❖ Suppliers with the same or similar names
- ❖ Purchases that were a mistake

Finding these problems would take many person-hours without the use of artificial intelligence (AI).

Artificial intelligence (AI) may also be used for market expansion in procurement. For example, it may forecast market pricing for your products, look for and find new suppliers, and evaluate any current ones you have as well. Your contract discussions will probably be more accessible and successful if you have a complete picture of these procedures.

Finally, AI may be used to collect monthly, daily, or automated hourly data in real-time. Procurement managers will be able to make choices more quickly and accurately as a result of this.

Expenditure Research

Spend analysis is one of the most frustrating aspects of procurement. However, managing risks and maximizing your organization's purchasing power is critical to your financial success.

When it comes to finding cost-saving possibilities, AI can help companies be proactive rather than reactive. It is only via thorough expenditure analysis that successful sourcing, category, and overall spend management strategies can be built upon. Data may be classified into functional, organized, and standardized categories using ML algorithms.

Insights on an organization's expenditures may be gained via AI-generated data. As a matter of fact, Deloitte estimates that the AI-generated expenditure categorization is 97% accurate. Good news for the purchasing sector.

Management of contracts

In the procurement process, Contract Management is critical and must be appropriately managed. However, dealing with contracts with all of the company's key partners may be time-consuming and challenging at times because of the legal language and implications you have to wade through.

According to a study published in the Harvard Business Review, companies may lose up to 40% of their value due to poorly managed contracts. This is because of things like:

- ❖ Acquiring familiarity with many contracts
- ❖ Differences in the way things are stated

In the company, there are varying degrees of compliance and expectations of value at various levels.

The contract administration process still requires human input and analysis, even though it has undergone considerable digitization in the past. Unfortunately, this obliterated all of the benefits that companies had hoped to get from this approach.

It is possible to automate terms and conditions management, deadlines, and anything else that requires monitoring by using natural language processing (NLP). Companies like Simfoni, which use AI technologies, can help you automate contract administration tasks.

Detection of Error

Some mistakes are just too obvious for a person to make. In your marketplaces, pricing fluctuations, compliance problems, and even fraud may be detected automatically by AI.

Manual jobs are becoming automated.

The procurement procedure includes many time-consuming activities. Artificial intelligence (AI) may automate formerly labor-intensive manual activities, such as receiving, verifying, and paying invoices, saving time and money. Artificial intelligence (AI) may also help with the procure-to-pay (p2p) process, which takes an average of nearly a month to complete manually.

Chatbots

A chatbot is a text-based program that initiates conversations with website visitors. Answering inquiries, getting as much information about the issue as possible, and adequately pointing people are all help desk goals.

Procurement assistants, such as chatbots, are capable of mimicking and adapting to human speech and writing. They combine natural language processing (NLP), video, audio, and imaging for interactivity with people. They want to make it easier for people to communicate with computers by personalizing the interaction. When given increasingly challenging tasks, it is designed to learn and identify patterns so that it may better interact with the environment.

The chatbot must have a thorough grasp of human linguistic meaning and context for this conversation to occur. Semantic analysis, i.e., the interpretation and analysis of the context in the surrounding text or words, is designed to operate via this. The AI examines the text structure in an effort to determine the correct meaning of words that may have several definitions.

A company's procurement systems may utilize chatbots for a variety of tasks. Employees, suppliers, and customers may all benefit from it since it can help with the grunt work of running the business. The chatbot can handle whatever data you provide, including stock availability, contact information, pricing, and supplier information. Because it's accessible all the time to answer your questions, you'll never be without access to critical information like order status or shipping inquiries again.

Despite considerable progress in this area, chatbots aren't yet ready to take the place of real humans in all situations.

Buying Suggestions from a Professional

Procurement is an integral component of almost every function in a typical company. Unfortunately, when given this duty, many workers wind up putting in long hours on menial jobs.

Determining the best rates, creating contracts, and locating reliable suppliers may all take a lot of time and effort. They've also been thrown away in some file system since neither side has the time nor energy to look for them. Off-contract expenditure is a potential hazard in this procedure.

AI seeks to solve this problem by providing guided purchasing by directing all employees to appropriate purchasing channels. There will usually be a series of queries included in the AI's algorithm. A user must answer a series of questions before the appropriate procurement channel can be reached.

One-time transactions create fewer disruptions when using artificial intelligence (AI).

Due to its capacity to handle large numbers of transactions flawlessly, artificial intelligence can minimize the disruption caused by one-off purchases. However, when a one-time purchase is made, this oddity often stops the procedure, which sometimes results in mistakes being recorded.

As a result, even if you need to utilize a provider once, AI will ensure everything goes well.

Managing the Risk of Suppliers

Supplier risk management is an excellent use of artificial intelligence in procurement. Artificial intelligence can detect unexpected changes in a supplier or a vendor correctly and rapidly and then determine if the shift raises or reduces risk.

Traditionally, this procedure would be reactive, but with artificial intelligence, the system can assist you in quickly weeding out providers that pose a safety concern. You don't have to deal with the hassles of having a long-term connection with these suppliers or providers. As a result, artificial intelligence has become a critical component of contemporary e-sourcing strategies.

Management of Stocks

The procurement industry relies heavily on inventory management. Traditional techniques are labor-intensive and expensive, necessitating a large number of people. To make the most of your available storage space, artificial intelligence can determine the inventory methods that are most effective for your particular company model.

Artificial Intelligence's Impact on Procurement

It's impossible to ignore the effect of artificial intelligence on procurement and how things are done as a result. Even yet, every new disruptive technology is fraught with dangers. Artificial intelligence (AI) in procurement is shrouded in misconceptions. To understand how disruptive AI has been to the industry, we must first debunk certain common misconceptions.

Dispelling procurement AI impact misconceptions

Myth 1: Artificial intelligence would result in fewer demands on human resources.

Whenever artificial intelligence (AI) is launched, the first concern on everyone's mind is: Will it replace me? Granted, these concerns are legitimate owing to the fact that humans have lost their value in the workplace as a result of AI. Fortunately, when we look at the whole procurement sector, this is not the case.

However, it's important to note that eliminating menial jobs would reduce the number of tactical positions accessible to those with less education and experience. The good news is that critical people may be readily redirected to other areas to counterbalance this. Artificial intelligence in procurement can do a wide range of tasks. It can't, however, completely replace human cognitive and emotional thinking capacity.

Myth 2: Artificial intelligence has a steep learning curve.

Adopting new methods of doing things and new technologies, particularly technology, has never been easy. It explains the procurement industry's slow adoption of artificial intelligence (AI) until recently.

There will be a steep learning curve for any new procedure. This is especially important if the procurement process entails switching from an old, inefficient method to a new, more efficient one. Although the learning curve will be steep at first, it should become less so as technology advances. However, it's important to note that eliminating menial jobs would reduce the number of tactical positions accessible to those with less education and experience. The good news is that critical people may be readily redirected to other areas to counterbalance this. Artificial intelligence in procurement can do a wide range of tasks. It can't, however, completely replace human cognitive and emotional thinking capacity.

Myth 3: Managing AI takes a lot of effort and money.

AI may be costly to set up, depending on the procurement process' complexity; nevertheless, prices will drop substantially beyond this point. Financing your company's growth by investing in artificial intelligence (AI) is a smart move. To the question of whether AI takes up a lot of time, the answer is emphatical no! In fact, we've repeatedly emphasized AI's potential to reduce time-consuming activities as a key advantage.

Myth 4: Artificial intelligence (AI) is still under development. Therefore it's best to wait before jumping on board.

If the epidemic taught us anything, it would be this. It follows, therefore, that when used properly, technology may be our greatest friend. Unfortunately, due to social distance and travel restrictions, procurement has been severely impacted. Unless something drastic happens, it's fair to say that things will never be the same again.

That being stated, it's apparent that we should get on board with artificial intelligence immediately. In many cases, procurement companies lose market share to rivals that have already integrated AI into their procurement operations. Furthermore, the AI available now is more than capable of significantly affecting your company, regardless of future upgrades and modifications.

Myth No. 5: Using artificial intelligence (AI) is difficult.

The opposite is true since artificial intelligence (AI) is designed to integrate with any current program or platform easily. Therefore, using AI in your operations does not need starting from scratch or creating new infrastructure.

How Artificial Intelligence (AI) Will Affect Procurement in 2022

The majority of industry professionals believe that the way AI is perceived has changed significantly, particularly in the procurement sector. Most businesses will begin with the applications we mentioned in our section on 'What are AI applications in procurement and sourcing?'

A fresh perspective on AI in procurement has emerged, however. As a starting point, many in the business now consider procurement to be more than simply an administrative process for transactions. As a result, we're witnessing a movement away from concentrating on low-risk supplier relationships and cost-effective purchases toward a more strategic approach.

What are we trying to say here?

It's becoming more and more common for procurement to be seen as a high-value addition to the company by concentrating on real-time analytics, intelligence, high spend visibility, minimal tail-end expenditure, and continual progress on cost-saving goals

Artificial intelligence (AI) is seen as the digital lever capable of producing such beneficial outcomes throughout the procurement spectrum.

Advantages of artificial intelligence when it comes to altering sourcing and procurement

By now, we're probably starting to sound like a broken record. However, we do not want to undervalue the advantages of AI in the procurement sector. Artificial intelligence has incredible capabilities that no other technology can match.

A Harvard Business Review and Deloitte research looked at the key areas where procurement companies may expect to experience the most significant advantages from the application of artificial intelligence (AI). Each company, of course, has unique difficulties and possibilities.

However, the results of the research indicated that the following key areas were the most likely in any company to benefit from AI:

- ❖ Relationships with suppliers: AI can improve the management of relationships with suppliers and discover new ones.

- ❖ New markets: Artificial intelligence (AI) makes it easy for businesses to sift through massive amounts of data, searching for new possibilities.

- ❖ AI helps companies make better decisions by providing them with precise analytics and data-based insights.

- ❖ AI streamlines complicated corporate processes with little impact on current infrastructure.

❖ AI can automate manual activities, which frees up resources and improves efficiency.

❖ Data Acquisition: AI enables any company to get access to vital new external data.

Procurement AI best practices implementation methods

Even though we've given you a ton of information on AI in procurement, the easiest way to get started is to take the first step. After that, we were using artificial intelligence (AI) in your procurement procedures doesn't have to be complicated.

The first step is, to begin with, the simplest of assignments.

Going all-in at once may sound exhilarating. However, if AI in procurement is not correctly deployed, it may soon become a tangled mess. Take a close look at all of your company processes and identify any routine or simple activities that may be automated using artificial intelligence (AI). If you incorporate AI into your current workflows, you'll likely see a return on your investment.

Step 2: Make sure you've gotten as much information out of it as you can.

Inaccurate or out-of-date data exacerbate an inefficient procurement process. However, capturing excellent data isn't absolutely necessary while you're just getting started. The goal should be to provide the AI with as much data as possible so that it can analyze and learn from it. Before launching your new AI program, be sure you've extracted as much as possible.

Step 3: Do not assign your AI duties that are difficult or ambiguous.

At this point, procurement AI is capable of handling a wide range of complex tasks. Even yet, if the challenge or instruction isn't clear, the technology may be unable to provide. For example, AI may readily navigate use cases such as classifying procurement expenses based on invoice data. However, it is unlikely that artificial intelligence (AI) would be able to replace human negotiators in high-stakes contract discussions fully.

Step 4: Don't forget to allow for feedback from others.

Despite its numerous capabilities, there are still limits to what AI can accomplish, particularly in the procurement process. To make the procedure as smooth as possible, you'll have to work with the technology occasionally.

AI Procurement Software from Simfoni

As a result, you've undoubtedly come to appreciate the potential of artificial intelligence (AI) software in the procurement process. With so many options available, finding software that's right for your company may be a challenge.

Software that Tracks Spend with the Help of Artificial Intelligence

We can customize our expenditure analytics software to meet the specific needs of your company. You may pick and choose whatever modules you want to use and discard the rest. You can coordinate the entire savings lifecycle in addition to attractive dashboards for visualizing spending. The purchase process may be made more profitable by selecting from one of our many modules.

The Verdict

There is no avoiding the fact that artificial intelligence is here to stay. Instead of fighting the changes, the most effective strategy is to accept them because artificial intelligence (AI) will change procurement, whether you like it or not.

In what ways is the world being digitalized?

Gartner describes the process of transitioning to a digital company as "the use of digital technology to alter a business model and offer new revenue and value-producing possibilities. "

A more technical approach incorporating digital tools into daily activities at both the individual and organizational levels has emerged over the last several decades as companies strive for more accessible and transparent data, quicker procedures, and increased productivity.

Digital Transformation is becoming a priority for companies since old static methods are no longer an option.

To describe how businesses emphasize IT modernization and digital optimization to build better business models that help rediscover and fulfill core consumer requirements, digitalization rapidly gave rise to "Digital Transformation/DX."

While it may seem difficult to grasp, Digital Transformation is now a process that every contemporary business has either begun or has already executed. The luxury brand Lolo Chatenay teamed together with the digital company Hapticmedia to create a more straightforward 3D visualization and setup demonstration.

Are you ready to utilize 3D configuration technology as Guerlain, Baume, Kenzo, and others use for better conversion rates? Get a free quotation from Hapticmedia by contacting them now!

According to TechPro Study, 70% of businesses have or are working on a digital transformation plan. At the same time, the IDG Digital Business research indicates that 44% of enterprises have entirely embraced a digital-first business approach.

There are many cautions concerning the dangers of digitization for people who aren't sure.

In the twenty-first century, digitization has become essential for every business hoping to succeed. Unfortunately, delays in responding to digitalization have the potential to bring down even the largest of organizations, as the COVID-19 disaster demonstrated.

Neiman Marcus, Bergdorf Goodman, Mytheresa, Horchow, and Last Call are a few examples of high-end retailers. Consumers' interest in digital experiences and online content is on the rise.

Digitalization is critical for companies since customers are constantly changing their purchasing habits and expectations.

Approximately 60% of the world's population is online, with 5.19 billion people using mobile phones. This information comes from WeareSocial and Hootsuite in their report Digital 2020. Over the course of the last year, 298 million new users, many of whom are from developing countries, have joined the internet.

In today's world, the average internet user spends 6 hours and 43 minutes per day browsing the internet, engaging in social media, using apps, and taking advantage of online services such as shopping and streaming. In addition, according to Nielsen research, digital consumption may rise by 60 percent or more during quarantine. Even in Hong Kong, a market dominated by brick-and-mortar stores, customers quickly adapted and began using e-commerce apps.

The social media platforms for sharing news about COVID-19 cases and related regulations multiplied in Asia, the first region affected by it.

Digital Transformation investments by companies are on the rise

As a result, companies worldwide invest in the digital transformation of their business models, customer and channel engagement, and products and services.

Digital technology investment is expected to rise between 15 and 20 percent, according to International Data Corporation, while digital transformation spending totaled more than $1 trillion in 2018.

In what ways does a successful digital transformation include the following elements?

Primary Foundational Elements: A new business model to innovate and capture value through digital channels

The Digital Enterprise, as a source of Experimentation, gives way to change. According to a study conducted by the World Economic Forum in partnership with Bain and Company, traditional approaches to today's business and operational goals are too linear and static.

It was agreed by the group's members that companies must have aspirational views of the future to establish a course of action, as well as increased flexibility to pivot and evolve. This means that flexibility, speed, and parallel development are essential. These can be achieved through digital strategies and tools that simplify decision-making, communication, implementation, and flow.

Digital Strategy is critical, but it won't get you very far if you don't have the right tools. A business model serves that purpose. An organization's value creation, delivery, and capture strategy are described as the rationale behind these activities.

Customers and channel engagement, products, services, operations, culture, and talent should all be part of a digital enterprise's business model.

The second pillar is a better digital customer service experience.

Neiman Marcus, a well-known retailer, has had a hard time going digital despite its efforts to improve the customer experience through the use of technology. Due to challenges implementing a cross-channel marketing system, the company suffered a $55 - $65 million loss in 2017.

Brands and customers alike have benefited greatly from digital platforms.

Online luxury sales, for example, have grown in popularity in recent years as basket values and numbers have both increased, contributing to a growth of 39% in overall luxury sales.

China has played a key role in the retail transformation and cannot be properly discussed without bringing up eCommerce. The Chinese e-shopping retail market has 650 million users and was valued at $1.5 trillion in 2019, making it more significant than the following ten markets combined. Moreover, Chinese consumers have adopted e-commerce at a rate of 64%, making it the world's largest e-commerce market.

Customers expect a personalized and engaging shopping experience and products that are specifically designed for them.

Brands such as Guerlain, Baume, and Kenzo have turned to 3D configuration technology to increase conversion rates. Get a free quote from Hapticmedia by contacting them today!

Brands like Guerlain have seen a twofold increase in conversions by allowing customers to design their lipstick via direct-to-consumer channels. In addition, Hapticmedia's 3D configurator lets make-up customers see what their final product will look like before placing an order.

More digital tools and technologies drive the new shopping experience, which involves less direct contact with salespeople.

Scientists say we should get used to living with COVID-19 before facing any new crises in the coming months and years. In other words, businesses will have to use digital tools to communicate and engage with customers instead of relying on personal interactions.

Artificial intelligence (AI) and big data are becoming increasingly popular for handling customer inquiries and complaints and making proactive product recommendations.

Baume, a high-end watchmaking company, uses virtual try-on technology to affect its multi-channel marketing strategy significantly.

Even so, there's more we can do. For example, consumers can now find products that best suit their tastes and needs thanks to new e-commerce technologies like virtual fitting rooms, 3D product configuration, try-on technology, live streaming, immersive reality, and mass customization.

Offering cutting-edge digital products and services is the third pillar.

Customers expect brands to keep up with the demands of the digital environment and provide convenience as more customers go online. According to a National Retail Federation survey, 83% of consumers now value comfort more than they did five years ago. Furthermore, retailers benefit from this feature because 97% of respondents said they abandoned a purchase due to inconvenience.

As a result of modernization, digitalization now has a home. According to estimates from 2013, the sharing economy had a value of $15 billion, significantly lower than the traditional operating model's value of $240 billion. But by 2025, the two are expected to equalize, each reaching a market value of $335 billion.

Brands will need to adapt to the growth of location-based computing, product configuration, chatbots, virtual try-on, IoT, and cloud services.

The use of smart home technology is also on the rise, with the International Data Corporation projecting that 1.39 billion devices will be shipped by 2023 in the United States alone. Companies like Amazon, Google, Apple, and Samsung have built extensive internet of things and smart-home platforms in the West. At the same time, the Chinese market is dominated by companies like Baidu, Alibaba, and Xiaomi. As a result, modern technologies such as smart TVs, smart speakers, robotic vacuum cleaners, lighting, and thermostats have become commonplace in consumers' lives.

New entrants are also getting involved and developing cross-compatible products and services, even though big players lead innovation through technology investment. Moreover, the pace of innovation is increasing. As a result, digital evolution is a never-ending process driven by customer needs.

Pillar 4: Operational, process, and system transformation

There is a rapid shift taking place in the global business landscape. This is due to the rapid advancement of technology, which is enabling previously unimaginable possibilities.

Robotics, the internet of things, smart factories, augmented reality, big data, and 3D printing are just a few of the technologies reshaping the way companies make products and the way customers search for, engage with, and shop for them. Advanced human-machine interfaces are also changing.

With all of these changes, Industry 4.0 has emerged, characterized by digitization in manufacturing and computerization throughout the entire supply chain.

Impacts: new technologies have increased levels of automation, customization, and productivity.

Ultimately, companies' desire to digitize as many parts of their business as possible using breakthrough technologies such as artificial intelligence (AI), machine learning (ML), and big data fuels digitization and integration of vertical and horizontal value chains, product and service offering portfolios, and business models and customer access.

We want to reduce our dependence on human workers while increasing profits and production. Therefore, we want to automate as many aspects of our companies as possible so that we can respond to customer preferences quickly and have machines learn on their own.

Digital culture is being fostered, as is the recruitment of digital talent.

Digital transformation isn't just about technology; it's about people and how they view it. Thus, a robust digital culture is considered a key driver of Digital Transformation.

It's critical to recognize that employees approach technology differently to create an environment or culture that encourages digitalization. Some people are fervently committed, while others are unsure or even apprehensive. They all require assistance on their journeys. In this case, a well-thought-out communication strategy should be in place.

Business units and IT departments need to work together to develop digital capabilities, and companies must create a business relationship management structure supported by digital talents to make this happen.

Making a solid digital culture also involves encouraging people's openness and willingness to accept the concept of Digital Transformation by demonstrating that technology is not an end in itself but a tool that aids businesses in streamlining processes, improving results, and achieving their objectives.

Examples, case studies, or an analytical approach to tasks can all be used to demonstrate this.

The more employees realize that new technologies like artificial intelligence, the internet of things, big data, and analytics are there to help them save time and improve deliverables rather than endanger their jobs or the working environment, the more willing they will be to embrace this digitally-savvy strategy will be to adopt it themselves.

We expect marketers to play a key role in driving digital transformation.

According to Forrester's To Get a Seat at the Table, Command Your Customer's Experience report, CMOs are less likely than their C-suite peers to be digital transformation leaders.

This is significantly less in comparison to technology leaders like IT managers, CIOs, and CTOs — or even CEOs, COOs, and CFOs — who are involved in strategy at a rate of 29% and execution at a rate of 16%.

What's concerning is that when digital transformation is left to CIOs or IT departments, the emphasis shifts away from satisfying customer demands and toward improving efficiency and optimizing resources. One of the cornerstones of digitalization is being overlooked here.

Customers expect brands to use digital tools to create authentic, inspiring, and engaging customer moments that are orchestrated and coordinated across all media. This is known as "the martech shift."

Customers must be satisfied and loyal for them to create a core competitive advantage. Therefore, they must also streamline processes.

CHAPTER THREE

WHAT IS A SUPPLY CHAIN?

In a supply chain, everything from sourcing raw materials through the final distribution and sale of the product is included.

Successful supply chain management may provide you with a competitive advantage over your competitors.

Recognizing and Appreciating the Supply Chain

A supply chain connects the point of origin to the end of consumption, and each link in the chain is referred to as a step along the way.

The raw materials are transformed into finished goods, which are subsequently sent to their ultimate destination, i.e., the consumer, for consumption.

The supply chain includes everyone from manufacturers to suppliers to inventories to warehouses to transportation firms to distribution centers to retailers.

The Supply Chain's Stages

The supply chain has a number of moving parts, as follows:

- ❖ The first stage in the supply chain is the extraction of raw materials.
- ❖ Refining or producing raw materials into fundamental components is step two.
- ❖ The third stage involves turning raw materials into final goods.
- ❖ The completed goods are sold in the fourth stage.
- ❖ It's time for the fifth phase, which deals with distributing completed goods to customers.
- ❖ Sixth, customer service and return services are discussed.

The following actions must be completed to carry out the steps as mentioned earlier:

- ❖ The supply chain relies heavily on documentation and agreements.
- ❖ Another essential aspect of moving things is physically moving those items from one location to the next.
- ❖ A place to keep things while waiting for them to be used
- ❖ Tracking and managing inventory and stock
- ❖ Management of demand and supply
- ❖ Tracking and verifying the authenticity of the merchandise
- ❖ Logistics and final-customer distribution

It is called supply chain management to create, manage, and optimize a supply chain. All parties engaged in the process are responsible for providing timely and correct information to help reduce problems and streamline the process.

Models of the Supply Chain

The following are a few different kinds of supply chain models:

Models for Continuous Flows

The continuous flow model, a classic supply chain design, is the ideal choice for producing commodities. Producing the same kind of product with little to no change on a regular basis benefits producers.

Models with a Short Supply Chain

The fast-chain approach is ideal for producers whose goods constantly evolve to keep up with the current fashions. It's perfect for a company that has a lot of new goods all the time. This paradigm is often referred to as the flexible model.

Models for Efficient Chains

An efficient chain model may provide businesses with a competitive advantage over their rivals. Therefore, the goal of this design is to be as efficient as possible.

Models That Can Be Fully Customized

The custom customized approach combines an agile and a continuous flow model, is best suited for goods with various options.

The continuous work model manages processes before product configuration, while the agile supply chain manages them after.

More Flexible Models

Businesses that deal with custom order goods benefit most from agile business strategies. Those that make goods with unpredictability in demand will do well with them.

Models That Can Be Adapted

The adaptable model is best suited for sectors with firm demand peaks followed by periods of low movement because it emphasizes excellent flexibility.

Manufacturers must emphasize adaptation and flexibility if they want this model to be a success.

Challenges in the Supply Chain

Supply chain managers have to deal with a wide range of issues. Here's what you'll see: Transparency is non-existent.

Owing to their obscurity, figuring out legacy supply networks may be challenging in some instances. As a result, commodities are more challenging to trace. A lack of openness may cause ineffective supply chain management and optimization.

Products Go Missing or Deteriorate

Streamlining the flow of processing products is one of the most challenging things to do. A lack of tracking may make it difficult to verify when items have been sent, received, and where they are — improper tracking.

An increase in waste, as well as a failure to plan properly

There may be a significant effect on productivity and profitability due to inefficiencies in the supply chain. For example, if status updates and reporting aren't correctly, supply chains will lose time, effort, and resources. As a result, it becomes more challenging to manage expectations and plans.

Obstacles stemming from differences in language

In the supply chain, the language barrier is a significant issue to be dealt with. Every country has its own official language that it uses to carry out its daily activities. Interpreters with experience and understanding of the business can help address these kinds of problems.

A comparison between supply chain management and business logistics

The words supply chain management, business logistics management, and logistics are frequently used interchangeably, so you should be familiar with them. That, however, is incorrect. These are two distinct concepts that must not be mixed together.

Logistics is primarily concerned with the organization of the storage and transportation of products and services from their point of origin to their final destination as part of the supply chain system. From raw resources to finished goods, it's a continuous cycle.

It's important to note that although supply chain management deals with managing a company's supply networks, logistics management focuses on the integration and upkeep of products inside the business. Supply chain management stresses competitive advantage, while logistics management promotes customer happiness.

What Is the Process for Moving Manufacturing Costs

Materials and labor are used to produce the final product, which may then be sold to the consumer. Therefore, this process is included in the flow of manufacturing expenses.

The manufacturing process's cost may be reduced using supply chain management. It also has the potential to simplify things.

Deflation and the Supply Chain

Supply networks have changed throughout time, contributing to the reduction of inflation. As the supply chain has become more efficient, the cost of transporting goods from one location to another has dropped, resulting in a lower-end product cost for the consumer. As a result, deflation has been caused by supply chain efficiency.

What's the Difference Between a Value Chain and a Supply Chain?

The value chain differs significantly from the supply chain. A value chain is a series of interconnected processes designed to increase the worth of raw resources so that finished goods may be sold to end-users. On the other hand, a supply chain is a system for making a product readily accessible to customers.

As a result, whereas the value chain concentrates on competitive advantage, the supply chain satisfies customers.

The best way to run a supply chain

It's not simple to be successful in today's hyper-competitive society. However, competitive advantage may be gained by your business by having an efficient and streamlined supply chain. The following are examples of effective supply chain management practices:

Supply Chain Management in Real-Time

The supply chain process may be more efficient if real-time supply chain planning is used. Historical data makes it harder to deal with disruptions, but a real-time supply chain makes it more accessible.

Utilize cutting-edge technology

The age of technology has begun in the contemporary period. Increase productivity and save expenses by implementing fully automated cross-functional procedures from start to finish. Strategic planning may be elevated to a new level by using the appropriate technologies, particularly sales automation and software solutions.

Focus on Building Better Relationships with Vendors

It's critical to have a good working connection with your vendor. If you want to keep your relationship, be sure you have a way to resolve disagreements.

Organize your Plan of Action

Strategic planning may boost operating expenses, improve quality across the supply chain, and decrease mistakes simultaneously.

The Supply Chain: Evolution and Prospects for the Future

Companies had to integrate business operations throughout the global supply chain because of globalization, outsourcing, and easy access to information in the 1980s and 1990s. As a consequence, supply chain management was born. As a result, the company used contemporary supply chain management instead of the old conventional supply chain. Because of the integration, there has been greater openness in the process.

The characteristics of market rivalry have changed significantly as well throughout the years. Instead of competing against one another, individual businesses, chains made up of many firms began to emerge. We also saw a shift in the way companies are operating in terms of outsourcing manufacturing and logistical functions to outside vendors.

As a result of this greater exposure, product traceability and social responsibility initiatives have both improved.. Once this was implemented in companies and consumers' daily lives, the internet of things and mobile computing completely changed commerce and company operations.

Direct communication with product distributors is now possible thanks to the internet. As a result, the supply chain's overall length has been cut in half. The COVID-19 epidemic, as it now exists, has altered the way people see the world. Inventory management and visibility have become more critical as a result.

Talking about machine learning and artificial intelligence in the future, these technologies will significantly impact diversifying the supply chain and improving response time.

To ensure that goods are delivered to customers promptly in the wake of the epidemic, economies may be under additional strain.

Procurement management may be defined as the management of purchasing.

A strategic approach to procurement is integrated via the use of procurement management. Procurement management's primary goal is to reduce the amount of money the company spends. In the procurement process, there are many steps: identifying a supplier, creating requests, placing an order, inspecting the supply received, issuing an invoice, and documenting the purchase process itself. It aids in the smooth operation of the company while also bringing about several additional advantages. Procurement processes that are well managed have a greater success rate and are more efficient. It also guarantees the organization's cost efficiency and savings. Procurement delays are the most difficult problem for a company to deal with. An efficient procurement process is required to avoid sourcing, purchasing, receiving, inspection, and billing delays.

What is the Importance of Procurement Management?

Every company is set up to generate profit. A company engages in many procedures while generating income. The supply chain is often the point at which the working process gets started. Creating a story for a procurement process may be difficult and time-consuming. The method itself is one thing, but putting it into action is quite another. Taking a plan from the drawing board to the actual implementation is a challenging task. As a result, it's critical to use procurement management's skills to their full potential. Procurement management protects companies and organizations from external threats.

The procurement process is a small component of the overall supply chain management process. The procurement process, on the other hand, is the backbone of a company's profitable operation. It's critical for the long-term viability of an organization, not simply significant. Therefore, purchasing management is crucial to a company.

Effortless operation

A process has two parts: planning and implementation. Planning is essential, but if it is not carried out properly, it may cause productivity and efficiency to be lost. As a result, the process is put under more stress. As a result, revenue creation and the company's long-term viability are put under pressure. The smooth operation of the company and organization is ensured by validated and significant procurement management. As a result, a company must make a considerable investment in the proper procurement procedure. To better grasp the role, effective procurement management:

❖ Decrease in the amount of manual work

❖ Pointing the way in a specific direction

❖ Productivity as a growth stimulant

❖ Providing services and resources to help the workers

❖ Examining the procedures and the overall process

All of these advantages are combined in a well-established procurement management system. It's in this way that a company with good procurement management may run smoothly.

Obtaining the necessary services

Procurement is the process of obtaining necessities for a company's operation, such as goods and services. An organization's goal in acquiring goods and services is to ensure seamless operation of the company and the creation of revenue-generating outputs.

The process that results in the final product uses both raw materials and services to make it easier to execute. The services that they generate workers and staff need. After then, the procurement group evaluates the situation and gets to work on the problem. Procurement management is critical in this situation. The top brass:

❖ Aids in determining whether or not a specific service is sufficient.

❖ Enabling cross-processing to improve functionality

❖ Locating and negotiating with vendors and service providers

❖ Providing the employees with a sufficient number of facilities

The service needs are prioritized in a well-researched and goal-optimized procurement management. To achieve the intended outcome, management effectively integrates all of the advantages into one package. Finally, the person receives the necessary services.

Saving money, time, and resources

When it comes to procurement, getting things like products and services is the most important goal. As well as reducing variable costs and time, the process emphasizes obtaining products and making effective use of resources. The productivity curve will remain steep if procurement management is genuine and validated. The investment will be based on how much the company can save in terms of money, time, and resources. Purchasing management will be in charge of:

- ❖ Make sure that the supply is properly negotiated
- ❖ Synchronization is essential for fast delivery and a comprehensive supply window
- ❖ Resource use that is both efficient and sustainable
- ❖ Process auditing elements made simpler

All of these advantages are available to a company with improved and highly effective procurement management. Effective procurement management is constantly optimized with a focus on saving resources such as money and time. Procurement management, together with the other elements, contributes to the advantages mentioned above.

Getting Rid of Mistakes

Manual labor is inherently error-prone. Every human-performed job carries with it the possibility of making mistakes. The fewer mistakes that are produced and documented, the more systemized and structured a process is. Procurement management may help to cut down on errors by doing some things. The purchasing department will be in charge of:

- ❖ Examine the delivery, the invoice, and the existing stock in detail.
- ❖ Improve outcomes by managing and rectifying the process as required.

❖ Workers in various roles cross-examining the procedure for inconsistencies.

Using Deskera Books, digitize the whole process. Fewer mistakes are cultivated when the purchase procedure is precise and step-by-step. Sourcing management starts with documents and works its way up to a finished product with pinpoint accuracy. This allows a business to carry out the procedure in a more precise manner. In addition, this aids an organization in identifying and correcting mistakes so that it can provide better outcomes in the future.

Keeping Timeliness as High as Possible

The value of time cannot be overstated. Wasted time is useless to any organization or company. Procurement management works with temporal accuracy to prevent the business from losing valuable time. Analysis of time consumption starts with generating orders and continues through the ordering and receipt of goods and the provider's payment. Purchasing administration:

❖ Determines how much time it takes to create the specifications

❖ Keeps track of and cuts order and supply times in half

❖ Inspection time is cut in half by following the procedure in a confirmed manner.

❖ Identifies how long the whole procurement process typically takes.

Procurement management will examine all of the factors before making a decision. To save time and speed up the churning process, the management has been improved. This saves the company money, labor and staff effort, and bad execution in the process.

Contracts that Pay Off Big Time

Contracts are often drafted to create legally binding connections and ensure both parties' safety. For the company, a contract provides delivery of orders, monetary agreements, time commitment, and many other elements of the relationship with the provider. In procurement management, it's critical to establish lucrative contracts to have good ties with suppliers. Contracts in procurement management may come in a variety of shapes and sizes:

- ❖ A one-time deal that lasts for a limited period
- ❖ Long-term – one-off agreement
- ❖ Long-term, as in a multi-year agreement

Contracts have a positive impact on both parties' sense of security. That, however, is not the case. Instead, contracts ensure that a steady stream of dependable supply of the business's needs is always available.

Procurement Management: The Key Steps to Success

The job of management is complicated since it involves many different processes. The management of tasks will be ineffective if there are no or few procedures. It's the same with procurement management. Managing a high-end procurement process properly becomes essential when your business wants to achieve it as efficiently as possible.

Procurement management requires the following stages to be completed successfully: These will assist you in fully comprehending and implementing the whole management process.

Creating and Organizing Requirements

A requirement creation process is a first and most crucial stage in procurement management:

- ❖ Assessing where the need is can help you get the process started right away.
- ❖ Plan a procedure for determining the needs and consumption of a product.
- ❖ Set up a procedure for drafting the requisite.
- ❖ Plan the next step in the evaluation of the draft requirement.

The last step is to create a mechanism for keeping track of how long it takes to produce a requirement draft and how long it will take to generate the next requirement draft after that.

Finding a Reliable Vendor

Finding a reliable supplier necessitates knowing where the next batch of supplies will come from. There are a few procedures involved in this phase, including as

Set up an inquiry with a request for proposals.

Start a procedure to determine the maximum amount of supplies a provider can offer effectively. To begin, determine your budget and the provider that best meets it. Finally, get in touch with the vendor and learn about their strategy to supply.

Deal-making and Contract-Building Negotiations

The procurement process necessitates the use of negotiations to reach an agreement. A procurement procedure aims to reduce costs to the absolute minimum. As a result, bargaining is no longer an option. The next stage is to create a contract that protects both parties involved in the process. To negotiate, you'll need to use certain procedures.

Figuring Out The Market Price For The Size You Need

Putting a stop to negotiations

Signing a formal agreement that contains all of the terms and conditions previously mentioned

Ordering

Simply placing an order requires some steps. First, the supplier receives the order list after the discussions. Next, the provider is required to take a certain amount of time when provided by the business. After that, the supply is delivered to the business. Without much work on the part of a business, the process concludes here.

Inspection of the supply is made available

Following receipt of the supply, this procedure is initiated. Analysis of the management and process's effectiveness for a company involves many procedures. These are the procedures that are employed:

- ❖ The process of registering for the supply to be received
- ❖ determining how much time it takes
- ❖ a complete review of the supply chain
- ❖ examining the supply chain for inaccuracies
- ❖ Putting the supply on the table for consumption after processing it
- ❖ Invoice Checking

The last step is to send out invoices. The procedure does not, however, stop with the billing. Although issuing an invoice seems to be a simple process, the finance team must thoroughly examine the invoice. Therefore, an examination of the invoice should be performed first, and then it may be authorized. The invoice inspection procedure comprises the following steps:

- ❖ Examining each item on the invoice to look for mistakes
- ❖ if there are any fake/default entries, check for them
- ❖ Manual synchronization of the invoiced supply
- ❖ Invoice final clearance by the purchasing and finance teams
- ❖ Payout at the end of the day

The payment is the process's last and most important step. The supplier produces an invoice once the transaction is complete. The finance department received this invoice. Before authorizing an invoice, the finance department does a comprehensive review.

Once the contract or procedure has been authorized, the finance team begins paying the supplier and puts an end to it. The agreement may go further, but it's not a given.

In what ways does Procurement Management seek to achieve its goals?

Procurement's primary goal is to reduce costs while still meeting the company's needs most conveniently and traditionally possible. The central procurement management goal is to process a flawless procurement system. You are deriving from the same.

Procurement management is intertwined with other aspects of an organization's operations. Some of the ecosystem's goals are significant, while others are more modest. Staff or company objectives may be used to frame these goals. Listed below are some of the most important goals that you and your company can't afford to overlook.

Purposes of Procurement Administration

Affordability

The primary goal of procurement management is unquestionably the establishment of cost-efficiency. A well-structured procedure using low-cost techniques can get you far. As a result, the company can create more while spending less money, ultimately leading to higher profits.

An established cost-effective management system allows the company to spend that same amount of money, increasing labor and employee productivity.

Operational Efficiency

Many stages go into the procurement process, all working together to achieve a common objective. Procurement management's goal is to make sure that all of these procedures go forward quickly and error-free as feasible. The goal of procurement management is to make operations run more smoothly. As a result, each process step concludes with a solid foundation upon which the following process may build.

Delivering on Promises

Any operation may be carried out in one of two ways. One approach is to perform it only as a means to complete a job. The other is putting out all of their effort to provide the necessary value for a company.

Procurement management aims to achieve corporate objectives while operating a slowed operation procedure. As a result, organizations, workers, suppliers, and customers all benefit from the value management creates.

Sourcing in a Sustainable Way

Who provides the product or service? From whence does the supplier get his supplies? Strictly how does it come into being? Do you think it's a human rights violation? Is it taking advantage of a person or a company? If so, where does it come from? Is it causing any damage to the environment?

Some issues arise while trying to locate a source of supply. It is the responsibility of procurement management to make sure that all sourcing is done ethically. The management checks the supplier's and supply sources' histories to ensure no illegal activities occur throughout the process.

Achieving Organizational Objectives in an Ethical Manner

Many objectives go into the formation of an organization. These objectives are all met thanks to procurement management. In addition, procurement management checks to see that all procedures are being followed lawfully.

Multi-tiered business objectives need sourcing from other sources. It is the responsibility of procurement management to make certain that the sourcing is done ethically as well.

There are many reasons why companies should digitize their procurement management processes. The goal of every company is to make a profit. The less profit a company earns, the more mistakes it makes. The company must guarantee error-free procurement management if it is to reduce procurement management mistakes.

If you're doing physical work or manual management, you're going to make mistakes. Unfortunately, the paper-based procurement management method does not meet this standard and should be avoided. Instead, businesses must digitize their management to guarantee a quick, seamless, and rapid procurement process.

With the digitization of the procurement process, everything from integrating inventory categories to checking supplier invoices is under control. In addition, the computerized method is faster, more accurate, and less expensive than the manual one. So, if you're a company owner, you should think about moving to a digital procurement management system.

Process management becomes fully automated with digital procurement. Inventory, supply, invoicing, procurement performance, supplier performance, and many other factors are all tracked automatically.

The digitalized automated procurement management also aids companies in building stronger connections with their suppliers because of it. Adding value and advantages to the company may be accomplished in various ways via the digitization of the process. A company should engage in digitizing procurement management for the following reasons.

Procurement Management: Why You Should Digitize It

Implementation Costs of Free-For-All

A company's ability to generate a more significant gross profit depends on reducing inventory costs. It is necessary to raise inventory costs to achieve this. To develop a need and work with a low-cost inventory implementation method, digitize your process.

Removal of Unnecessary Spending

Manual processes tend to underestimate costs. As a result, there may be a distinct cost flow from the company that adds little value. Automated digital procurement management systems can identify and reduce waste.

Reducing the amount of time and money spent on production

Each procedure may be evaluated and analyzed thanks to digital procurement management. As a consequence of the investigation, a conclusion may be drawn. Procurement can see ways to save time and money by using this information. A company's profit margin is impacted differently as well.

Increased Accountability for Spending

With digital procurement management, everything is sorted for you on demand. Records and statistics are created and stored in a convenient location. This makes it simple to keep track of how much money is being spent. As a result, the team in charge of procurement management will have complete insight into budgetary expenditures. They may then alter their spending as necessary by increasing or decreasing it.

Increased Productivity

By digitizing the procurement process, several departments will be free of manual work. As a result, the process is well-defined, and the results are articulated. As a result, grasping the procedure is a breeze. As a result, the whole procedure is simple to comprehend and use. Thus, bringing it to a close by increasing efficiency at every turn.

Errors are being reduced.

Errors may occur when anything is done by hand, whether it's a job, a computation, or an analysis. On the other hand, a digital management system is fully automated and does not require much human labor. This aids the process's smooth operation by reducing the likelihood of mistakes.

Ways to Boost Procurement Management Efficiency

There are many goals in a procurement process. To achieve all of these goals, a company requires a well-defined procurement procedure. However, without effective procurement management, the process would be slowed to a crawl.

Procurement management can keep a company running, but only a top-notch procurement team can guarantee effective procurement management. In addition, procurement management is a complex process that involves many different activities. This may lead to miscommunication and operational problems. Procurement management must be efficient if it is to provide the best outcomes possible. Take a look at these seven suggestions for maximizing productivity.

Improvements in the Supplier Relationship

When it comes to the procurement process, suppliers are key players. A procurement manager will be surrounded by suppliers and should be in this position. When it comes to building a solid business connection with a supplier, it's critical to keep things cordial.

Improving ties with suppliers results in hassle-free, long-term business partnerships based on trust. Saving the company from frauds, mistakes, and unethical sourcing are all possible using this method.

Consider Your Purchases Before Making Them

The company's employees are tasked with creating a requirement draft that includes all of the necessary inventory and infrastructure. On the other side, it is up to the procurement team to decide which criteria it will meet. Thus, it saves the company money to go through the procurement procedure. However, the procedure also has the right to make a more informed purchasing choice.

To achieve greater efficiency, the procurement management team must make thoughtful acquisitions.

Establishing Negotiating Measures

A procurement manager's ability to negotiate is non-negotiable. Cost-cutting is the primary goal of a procurement procedure. The only way for a procurement team to save money is via bargaining.

Better relationships with suppliers and better supply may be obtained by negotiating on the appropriate conditions. Negotiations guarantee that the best price a company should provide is met by meeting the primary objective. Contract building and agreements are also part of the negotiation process.

Expansion of the Community

To be competitive, a company must continuously find new suppliers, dealers, and procurement team members. As a result, companies and purchasing managers will need to form a more comprehensive network. Procurement management may be enhanced and made more efficient by expanding one's professional network.

The network may be expanded via a variety of means. Use social media, current suppliers, rivals' suppliers, and relationships among employees, for example.

Make Use of Modern Resources and Technology

Manual processes take longer and cost more money than digital processes. Therefore, a company should invest in tools and technology to guarantee procurement management efficiency. A well-thought-out technical approach usually yields superior outcomes.

Tools make it easier to maintain operations and procedures well-organized and efficient while also saving time and money. However, to get more significant outcomes, a company must make investments in new technology and equipment.

Conducting Mock Training Sessions Regularly

When it comes to producing high-quality outcomes, more practice and better-trained employees mean more success. Mock training should be an essential part of this process. To ensure that employees have adequate experience and recognition of new technologies and facilities, conduct a mock training session.

Mock tests provide a chance to evaluate the process and make improvements based on what is learned from the results. As a result, every stage of the process and the whole management are more efficient.

Sourcing with a Strategy and a Timeline

When sourcing isn't planned and managed ahead of time, it may be problematic. Sourcing is a time-consuming procedure that benefits from a step-by-step approach. Calling for quotes is only the beginning; you'll also need to write the requirements, establish relationships with suppliers, and receive and check the supply.

Processes that are pre-planned and structured provide better results while generating fewer mistakes.

Procurement Management Should Be Automated

Procurement management practices remain primarily unchanged in the majority of businesses. If you're going through the same thing, you know how frustrating it may be. Procurement management that isn't automated quickly transforms into labor-intensive procurement management. This necessitates a great deal of time and effort on your part. In addition, the documentation of procedures necessitates a large amount of paper. As a result, there's more room for mistakes.

The use of manual procurement management creates an additional risk of fraud. Workers or vendors can conduct fraud. Humans tend to ignore or notice fraud. A computerized system examines every aspect of a situation minutely. All procedures are well handled, from the generation of the required draft until the start of payment.

A company should automate its procurement management for the following reasons.

Automating Procurement Management Has Many Advantages

Request for Quotation Forms in Digital Format

Streamlines communication between the procurement team and the supplier by making it easier to exchange needs and quotes.

Draft of Digital Requirement

Aids the procurement team's organization and orderly feed the staff's need to move the process forward.

Analyses and approvals made using digital technology

Procurement automation software does all the work and analyses on its own. The procurement team is responsible for keeping it up to speed with new information, but beyond that, the tools are self-sufficient.

Digital Supply Chain Monitoring

To guarantee that supplies comply with needs and use, automated procurement management is used.

Autonomous Verification of Billing Information

Inspection of invoices requires a sharp and focused eye. Even the most minor error may result in a significant loss for the company. Therefore, before authorizing an invoice, it is carefully examined using an automated procurement management procedure.

Sorting Out the Best Vendors

Data and supplier information may be analyzed by the automated tool. The tool may then choose the provider based on the specified criteria.

Lowering the Number of Errors

Errors may be reduced by eliminating manual tasks. For example, errors in the purchase process are almost eliminated with automated procurement management.

Savings in Money and Time

Technology and tools are used to conduct automated operations. This eliminates the need for a manual procedure and saves both time and money.

Increased Accountability for Spending

It's critical to have enough information to make an educated purchase and ordering choice.

Improved Process Control

Procurement automation allows for a more in-depth analysis of the process. Automated management will be able to take better steps to rectify and improve management if the process does not achieve intended outcomes.

What do the terms "plan purchases," "conduct purchases," and "administrate purchases" mean?

The administration of procurement is a complex procedure. First, a procurement team looks outside the group for individuals who can complete a task. The procurement team, for example, locates vendors, shippers, and customer service providers as required, among other things. Thus, managing the procurement process requires several levels of management.

Here's a breakdown of the procurement management process so you can see how everything fits together.

What does it mean to "plan purchases," "do purchases," and "administer purchases"?

Organize the Procurement Process

Procurement process planning entails simultaneously creating several procedures. The procurement team is in charge of ensuring that the needs of the company's employees and workers are fulfilled. To fulfill the need, the team will have to turn to third-party providers and vendors. The team must also perform inventory control checks to ensure they are fulfilling all criteria. During this stage of the procurement process:

- ❖ Organizing the need
- ❖ locating and evaluating potential suppliers
- ❖ highlighting the dangers that may exist
- ❖ Contracts for building work

At this point, procurement managers must improve their ability to establish and maintain effective working relationships. The next stage is to conduct a complete background check on all vendors. Finally, they must master the art of closing transactions by engaging in effective negotiating techniques.

The following stage is to compute the kind of contract to be created with the provider once the whole procedure has been planned. As soon as the contract is signed, it becomes an agreement between the company and the vendor that serves as a safety term and duty.

Carry out Sourcing

In this phase, the plan has to be put into action once it has been planned. Again, there are many steps involved in putting the plan into action. To carry out the plan, the team must participate in a series of activities that include

The Process Of Getting Vendors To Submit Bids

Solicitation of all relevant data from manufacturers and distributors.

Deciding On And Working With A Vendor

Performing research and developing contractual provision

The procurement team must keep track of all the data they've gathered. Future associations may find this helpful material. Additionally, the data may assist a company in building stronger ties with its community and supplier network. Furthermore, the data aids in a better understanding of customer and supplier needs.

The order is placed immediately once the need has been evaluated and contracts have been established.

Manage the Procurement Process

The final step in procurement management is administration. Execution is not a part of this phase of management. However, the administration of the process is included in this phase, as the name implies. It aids in devising new strategies in place of those that aren't yielding the intended outcomes. The following elements are included in this stage:

- ❖ Supply chain audit
- ❖ examination of the bill of sale
- ❖ a complete evaluation of the quality of the supplier
- ❖ An examination of the provider's efficiency
- ❖ a comprehensive examination of the whole procedure

Managing procurement is the phase in which the team may examine and, if necessary, correct the process and contracts. The goal is to keep the process running as efficiently as possible. During this phase, the procurement team makes sure that the purchase process is as efficient as possible.

Managing procurement also allows you to develop stronger ties with external suppliers and teams.

The Determination of Need

Identifying a company's need is the first stage in the procurement process. Next, the employees and labor recognize and enlist the need for inventory. Most companies still do this by hand, although many technologies are available to help streamline the process.

Creating a Draft of the Requirements

They create a draft of the inventory needed once it is ready to offer their demand. Requirements are double-checked by the procurement or inventory teams before being analyzed. The team then drafts a need that includes the amount, usage, and other information for the inventory and facilities described earlier in this document.

Assessments of Need

The procurement team receives a draft of the requirement. Before making a final decision, the procurement team weighs in on the draft by looking at inventory turnover, the necessity for inventory, and the inventory's productivity. Once the draft has been accepted, it will be sent to the finance department, determining how much money has to be allocated to meet the need.

Selection of Vendors

Finding and selecting a supplier is the most critical stage in the procurement process. First, the procurement team issues a request for quotes to various vendors about their wants and needs. After then, the bids are scrutinized closely to ensure they meet the specifications. Finally, following a background investigation and selection of a final provider, your team will have found your perfect supplier.

Term and Price Negotiation

A contract is negotiated between the company and the supplier once the provider has been chosen. After that, the company enters into negotiations with the supplier to work out pricing and budget. Once both parties have agreed on comparable conditions, a contract may be drafted to protect them both. As a result, the supplier and the company have a stronger working relationship.

Delivery Checkup

Receiving and inspecting the goods is the final stage in the procurement process. The procurement team will start to work as soon as the supplier has made the delivery. The crew checks the supply for quality, quantity, and any mistakes. This aids company in reducing unnecessary expenses and therefore saving money.

Approval and payment of invoices

The last and most crucial stage in the procurement process is the payment of the bill. The finance team inspects the invoice as soon as the company receives it from the supplier. The invoice is thoroughly checked in compliance with the received supply. As a result, the company saves money on unnecessary expenses. In addition, it safeguards the company from fraud and invoicing errors.

The finance department initiates the payment after the invoice has been authorized.

CHAPTER FOUR

BLOCKCHAIN TECHNOLOGY

Modern technology is advancing at an incredible rate, reaching new heights of accomplishment. The development of Blockchain technology is one of the most recent successes in this area. This new technology is having a significant impact on finance. In reality, it was designed specifically for use with Bitcoin, the digital money that made it possible. However, it has now found use in a variety of different contexts.

To have made it thus far was most likely a piece of cake. But, what exactly is Blockchain?

The use of a widely dispersed database

Consider a computer network in which a spreadsheet is replicated many times. Please assume that the computer network is so intelligently constructed that it automatically updates the spreadsheet regularly for the sake of argument. Hopefully, this has given you a better understanding of what Blockchain technology entails. The blockchain acts as a decentralized database for sharing information. Additionally, this information is updated regularly to account for any changes.

There are advantages to using this strategy over the conventional one. First, it prevents the database from being kept in a single place. Second, it contains authentic public documents that are readily verifiable. Third, unauthorized users cannot damage the data since there is no centralized version of the records. Finally, blockchain is a distributed database that is hosted by millions of machines simultaneously, making it available to virtually everyone on the virtual network.

It's a good idea to use the Google Docs comparison to help explain the concept or technology.

Blockchain as analog to Google Docs

To transmit a Microsoft Word document to many recipients as an attachment has been standard since the invention of the eMail. Before returning the updated copy, the receivers will take their sweet time reading it. This method necessitates waiting for the return copy before seeing the document's modifications. This occurs because the sender cannot make changes until the receiver has finished modifying the document and returned it to the sender. A current database does not permit the simultaneous use of the same record by more than one individual owner. Client or account balances are kept this way by banks.

On the other hand, Google Docs allows both parties to have simultaneous access to the same document. Additionally, it enables you to see the same document in two places at the same time. Google Docs is a lot like a shared ledger in that it's a document that everyone has access to. If many people are sharing something, the dispersed aspect comes into play. In a sense, Blockchain is an extension of this idea. The Blockchain, on the other hand, is not intended for the exchange of documents. It's just an example to give you a better understanding of this cutting-edge technology.

Essential characteristics of the blockchain:

- ❖ The blockchain is a distributed database that holds blocks of data that are the same all across the network. As a result of this characteristic:
- ❖ There is no way for a single organization to control the data or information.
- ❖ No single point of failure is also possible.
- ❖ There is complete openness in the process since the data is stored on a public network.
- ❖ The information contained on it can't be tampered with.
- ❖ Instability of the cryptocurrency market

It's no secret that Blockchain technology has a wide range of uses in the financial and banking industries. Only in 2015, over US$ 430 billion in money transactions were made using it, according to the World Bank. As a result, there is a large market for Blockchain developers.

In these kinds of monetary transactions, the Blockchain removes the commissions paid to intermediaries. The GUI (Graphical User Interface) made desktop computers more accessible to the general public. Also, with Blockchain technology, the wallet application is the most popular graphical user interface. When utilizing Bitcoin or another cryptocurrency, users make purchases using their wallets.

What does the term "blockchain" mean?

Many people have been talking about blockchain lately, and although it seems like everyone has heard of it, the majority of people have no clue what it means.

To better understand what blockchain technology implies, let us take a look back at the evolution of money transactions throughout time. There have always been middlemen involved in the trade of valuables whose only function was to verify the validity of both parties and foster a sense of confidence. Banks are the current name for these middlemen. However, as digital assets like shares, electronic money, and intellectual property have developed, a more secure approach has become necessary. Traditionally, banks and brokers have served this purpose. This is because digital assets are often stored as files on a computer, making them susceptible to theft and modification. Therefore, it is possible to do business in a safe, secure, efficient manner thanks to blockchain technology.

Bitcoin's Long-Term Prospects

As social media upset conventional media and as Netflix decimated Blockbuster films, blockchain has the potential to upend the financial sector. People in emerging nations, who may not have access to conventional banking services or who cannot pay the rates needed to conduct significant transactions, may be able to utilize blockchain technology as a platform to access financial services. It can make significant advances in almost all of the main sectors, even those that large companies often influence.

Teaching using BlockChain Technology

A student's ability to pay for tuition may be determined by using blockchain technology in education. This is due to a small number of students who have gotten financial aid outside of the established channels. This would harm the most vulnerable students, who would be forced to choose between finishing school or working to pay off their debt.

And last, even if a large portion of the public would want blockchain to disappear, it is clear that this is not the case. Eventually, we will all be trading on the blockchain as part of our everyday lives, and our great-grandchildren will read about money and ATMs the same way we did about barter trade and gold. As a result, we must hop on board the bandwagon as quickly as possible and make the necessary adjustments before we are forced to.

Trade finance is a good candidate for blockchain technology since it has a high adoption rate. In addition, research and development are a priority for many of the world's biggest banks.

R3CEV, a group of 71 global financial executives, has discovered much information regarding blockchain's possible applications.

R3 has conducted some market pilots to supplement their research since 2016. They'll keep refining their approaches until they're ready to join the market.

In other words, what are some of the things they learned that might be useful? With blockchain technology firms, here's what trade finance will look like in the future.

Constantly keep track of the current state of affairs and conditions

CBA, one of R3's members, has made significant contributions to blockchain technology research. They are currently working on three distinct blockchain-related projects.

They're trying it out on cotton exporters as a test. The canister contains a humidity sensor connected to the internet of things (IoT) and a global positioning system (GPS).

Customers may keep track of their shipments in real-time with this monitor. They may also keep tabs on the condition of their goods as they go through the system.

Other national blockchain technology firms are conducting similar studies. For example, Hellosent is conducting comparative trials in Singapore. They are, however, looking at the import of French wine at the moment.

- ❖ Resolve the Issue of Unpaid Claims

- ❖ Grain producers are increasingly concerned about the financial losses they suffer as a result of trade insolvencies. In 2014, this action resulted in a loss of $50 million.

- ❖ A farmer must wait 4-6 weeks before being paid for exports. Farmers and purchasers often clash over overpayment issues due to this (failing to pay the appropriate amount, late payment, etc.).

- ❖ Complete Profile, an Australian start-up, has decided to act on their own own.

- ❖ Farmers may now get paid upon the delivery of grains through their blockchain platform. Farmers and purchasers will be less likely to get into arguments as a result of this.

- ❖ As soon as Full Profile's domestic application fully functions, they will move on to international commerce.

Digitize

Reducing financial loss and risk may be made easier with the usage of blockchain. More advancements will allow for the digitalization of sales and legal contracts.

As a result, trade finance is a complicated field that depends mainly upon transactions like settlements and agreements. As of now, most of these agreements are executed on paper.

The paper-based method will be replaced with blockchain technology. As a result, the likelihood of financial loss is reduced since papers are often misplaced, damaged, or tainted.

The tracking of electronic documents is much more efficient. In addition, a third-party verification mechanism is not required.

When used in medical research, blockchain technology creates a permanent, time-stamped record of the results, increasing public confidence in the study's validity. Because of blockchain technology, transactions in a ledger cannot be altered over time, according to Satoshi Nakamoto's invention in 2008. Bitcoin (BTCblockchain)'s technology provides an immutable record of all transactions, making it impossible for anyone with authority to control the currency.

Due to the system's usage of a distributed database, it is more secure than traditional financial institutions' centralized databases, which are still in use today. To enhance confidence in medical research, this same technology may be used. This increases the permanence and immutability of the transactions (scientific data gathered).

A high degree of trust is required for both the exchange of money and the conduct of medical research. Government rules and central bank supervision have historically fostered confidence in money by using peer reviews performed by renowned medical publications like the New England Journal of Medicine. However, the trust may be generated in two ways: either via the government or through a medical publication that is well respected.

As a result, both techniques are very vulnerable to fraud, whether from organized crime or human mistakes. As a result, many people have lost faith in medical research. With Bitcoin, you may trust the distributed network rather than a central authority subject to human mistakes because of the mathematical process.

Transactions involving money require a high degree of confidence. Every transaction in the ledger must be wholly correct and impervious to future revisions since otherwise, the information would be useless. As a result of the public's confidence in bitcoin's use of blockchain technology, the digital currency has grown to a market valuation of over $100 billion. There is more than $250 billion in confidence placed in blockchain-based financial systems when other cryptocurrencies are taken into account, too.

Similarly, health care providers must have confidence in the accuracy and immutability of data acquired through medical research. Patients and doctors alike require assurances that medical research is neither plagiarized nor false in any manner. Bitcoin has now become a widely accepted worldwide currency thanks to the advent of blockchain technology. Similarly, medical research conducted using blockchain technology would enhance public confidence in the findings, resulting in better medical treatment.

Is Blockchain the Internet's Future?

Getting Rid of Reliable Third-Parties Is Difficult: Because of its potential to make each specific process, activity, and association fully self-governing, Blockchain, the unchangeable scrambled, decentralized record, is a game-changer. This means that we may get rid of third parties like mediators and experts and win back our confidence. Moreover, it is possible to streamline all of these aspects while yet maintaining their unique character and purpose.

As the house loan market fluctuates, a complex network of title checks, title protection, and many small exchange fees are needed to keep things moving. These structures are in place because exchanging land has always required much faith in historical documents. Although this is a concern, the Blockchain could alleviate it. The record of a specific property could contain a clear and approved history of exchanges, reducing the requirement for foundations to provide chance relief and put their trust in administrations. Instead, the exchange could exist on its right.

In 2018, blockchain technology advanced significantly since the introduction of Bitcoin.

The modest growth of Bitcoin in 2017 fueled the blockchain's long-term quality and favorable conditions, the critical advancement utilized by this sophisticated form of money. In 2017, blockchain became the second most common look term, and distributed record development will continue to gain significance across different sectors. In terms of financial theory, blockchain projects will beat those based on communicated figures and IoT. Furthermore, due to government blockchain initiatives like Malta's, local markets are likely to be driven.

Assuring Future Internet Security

Compared to alternative record programs, blockchain has the main benefit of being cryptographically dependent and updated to be unchangeable. This means that data cannot be changed by going back in time to a particular point on the blockchain. For the last ten years, blockchain has been impenetrable and will remain so for the duration of the technology's lifespan.

Digital advertising and the blockchain

Computerized advertising has some challenges to overcome, including space extortion, bot migration, a lack of transparency, and complex installation models. The problem is that incentives aren't changed, so both promoters and distributors feel like they're missing out on something. The blockchain is the solution to bringing transparency to the retailer's network since it implicitly instills confidence in an otherwise uncertain environment.

As employees, we've become so used to being paid every two weeks or so that it's taken for granted. However, the year 2018 marks the point at which this is no longer considered a necessary need. Miniaturized scale installations are one of the most energizing aspects of blockchain innovation. Another one is the ability to negotiate well under pressure. Various paths may be taken to connect them, including one that results in cash spillage. It was predicted years ago, but the reality is that it's just occurring the way everyone expects it to at this moment

In the end, blockchain is a fantastic technology for storing enormous amounts of essential documents in many endeavors, such as human services, coordination, copyright, etc. Moreover, when it comes to approving contracts, blockchain does away with the need for a middleman.

What is Blockchain Technology?

Let's suppose a new technology is invented that enables a real estate transaction to be transacted by multiple parties. The parties meet and finalize the specifics of the schedule, unique conditions, and funding. These parties will only know that they can rely on each other via some proof. A variety of third parties would need to be consulted to confirm the terms of their agreement. When it comes to saving money with technology, they're back where they started.

Third parties are now asked to participate in the real estate sale and provide their opinion while the transaction is formed in real-time. Thus, there is no longer any need for the intermediary. The intermediary may even be removed in certain instances if the transaction is thus open and honest. To avoid misunderstandings and litigation, the attorneys are always handed to help. These dangers may be substantially minimized if the conditions are stated upfront. There will be no surprises later on regarding payment, as long as the financing has been arranged in advance. The example is now complete. How will the transaction be paid for after all of the terms and agreements have been worked out? Since a central bank would issue the money, you'd have to deal with the banks again. If this occurs, banks will not allow these transactions to go through without doing some due diligence on their end, which will result in additional fees and delays. Have efficiency gains been achieved using this technology? It's doubtful to be the case.

Is there a remedy? Incorporate digital money into the transaction terms so that it's as transparent as the deal itself is. In such a case, all that's left is to convert the digital money into a well-known one like the Canadian or U.S. dollar, which may be done at any moment if it's interchangeable.

It's clear from the example that the technology being referenced is blockchain. Economic growth would be stymied without international trade. Money is essential for commerce because it allows people to exchange goods and services. Export and import activities and taxes account for a significant portion of regional activity. Any savings that may be made in this area and applied globally would have a significant impact. Consider the concept of free commerce as a case in point. Before free trade, nations would import and export with one another for a long time, but they had a tax structure that taxed imports to limit foreign products' impact on the local country. These tariffs were abolished due to free trade, resulting in the production of many more products. An even slight shift in trade regulations has a significant impact on global trade and industry. The term commerce can be split into more particular sectors like shipping, real estate, import/export, and infrastructure. It is more apparent how profitable the blockchain is if it can save even a tiny proportion of expenses in these areas.

Crypto-what?

For some who have dabbled with blockchain, the sheer obscurity of the technical language used to describe it is enough to turn back in fear. Before discussing what cryptocurrency is and how blockchain technology might transform the world, let's first define blockchain.

Just as the ledgers we've been using for centuries to record sales and purchases, a blockchain is nothing more than a digital ledger. This digital ledger serves the same purpose as a conventional ledger in that it records debits and credits between parties. In essence, that's how blockchain works; the distinction is in who manages the ledger and who validates the transactional data.

Tradition dictates that for payment from one person to another to be successful, there must be an intermediary involved. Think about the scenario where Rob wishes to send Melanie £20 through wire transfer. It's his choice to hand her a £20 bill in cash or use a banking app to send the money straight to her bank account through a mobile payment system. Rob's finances are confirmed when he withdraws cash from a cash machine or via the app when he makes a digital transfer, with a bank acting as the middleman in both instances. This is something that is left up to the bank's discretion. Rob's bank keeps track of all his transactions and is entirely responsible for keeping them up to date when he sends money to someone or gets the money. It's as if everything is funneled via a single financial institution.

As such, Rob must trust his bank to place his money there. Otherwise, he will not. He has to have complete faith that the bank would not cheat him, lose his money, or be robbed. During the financial crisis of 2008, when banks were shown to be reckless with our money, the government (another middleman) decided to bail them out rather than risk losing the last vestiges of confidence by allowing them to go bankrupt.

However, blockchains vary in one meaningful way regarding how they work: they are entirely decentralized. There is no central clearinghouse like a bank, and no one organization holds a central ledger. Instead, the ledger is replicated over an extensive network of computers known as nodes, each of which has a copy of the complete ledger on its hard drive. These nodes are linked by a piece of software known as a peer-to-peer (P2P) client, which synchronizes data throughout the network of nodes and ensures that everyone gets the exact version of the ledger at any given moment in time.

New transactions in a blockchain are encrypted using cutting-edge cryptographic technology before being added to the ledger as evidence. Once the transaction has been encrypted, it is turned into a block, a slang word for collecting encrypted new transactions in the system. Each node in the network verifies this block before passing it on to everyone else. Once confirmed, the block is then appended to the end of the ledger on everyone's computer, beneath the list of all previous blocks. It's the chain that's termed a blockchain because of this technology.

The transaction will be complete after it has been authorized and entered into the ledger. Currencies operate similarly, as shown here with Bitcoin.

The loss of confidence and increased accountability

A banking or central clearing system has many benefits over this one. For what reasons would Rob choose to pay using Bitcoin rather than fiat money?

Trust is the solution. Rob must have complete faith in his bank to safeguard and correctly manage his money, as previously stated regarding the financial system. These acts are verified and suitable for the purpose by massive regulatory systems, which exist to guarantee this. Governments then regulate the regulators, resulting in a tier-based structure of checks and balances whose only aim is to assist avoid errors and unethical behavior. For better or worse, organizations like the Financial Services Authority exist because banks cannot be trusted on their own. We've seen too many instances of banks misbehaving and making errors, as well. People tend to abuse or misuse power when there is just one authoritative figure. Although individuals have a tense and fragile trust relationship with banks, there isn't much of an option.

To put it another way: Blockchain systems are decentralized and need no trust on your part. There is no single point of failure or approval channel in a blockchain since all transactions (or blocks) are validated by the network's nodes before being added to the ledger. Hackers would have to simultaneously infiltrate millions of machines to alter a blockchain ledger effectively. To knock down the blockchain network, a hacker would have to shut down every single computer in a global network of computers, which is almost impossible.

Another important consideration is the encryption method used. For the verification method, blockchains like the Bitcoin one employ purposefully complex procedures. If you're using bitcoin, you're verifying blocks by solving riddles or solving complex mathematical problems, which takes a lot of time and resources. As a result, block verification is neither quick nor readily available to the general public. Instead, transaction fees and a bonus of newly-minted Bitcoins are awarded to nodes who dedicate resources to block verification. Because processing blocks like this takes sophisticated computers and much energy, this serves the dual purpose of incentivizing individuals to join the network while also managing the currency's generation process. Because it takes much work (by a computer) to create a new commodity, this is referred to as mining. Another benefit of decentralization is that transactions can be validated in a manner that would be impossible with government-regulated organizations like FSA.

To put it another way: Because of blockchains' self-regulatory character, they can operate without the intervention of a central authority figure, government, or another third party. They're effective due to a lack of trust among individuals rather than because of it.

Once you realize how significant it is, the enthusiasm around blockchain will begin to make sense.

Contracts using artificial intelligence

The uses of blockchain beyond cryptocurrencies like Bitcoin are where things become fascinating. It's simple to think of different uses for the blockchain system's safe, independent transaction verification, given that it's one of the system's fundamental concepts. Many of these types of applications are already in use or in development, which is not unexpected. The following are a few of the best:

Ethereum's smart contracts: Smart contracts are blocks of code that must be run to complete a contract, making them the most intriguing blockchain development since Bitcoin. As long as a computer can run the code, the code may be whatever you want, but in layman's terms, it implies that you can utilize blockchain technology to build an escrow system for any kind of transaction. Take web design as an example. If your client's website hasn't yet opened, you might establish a contract that releases the money to you automatically once it does. You won't have to bother with any further follow-up or billing. For example, property or artwork may be shown to be owned via smart contracts. This strategy has tremendous promise for minimizing fraud.

➢ Story cloud storage:

Cloud computing revolutionized the web and ushered in the era of Big Data, which in turn sparked a new wave of innovation in artificial intelligence. Nevertheless, most cloud-based services are provided by computers housed in a single data center (Amazon, Rackspace, Google, etc.). Because a single, opaque organization holds your data, it poses the same issues as the banking system. For example, it is impossible to bring down a blockchain network, thus distributing data on a blockchain eliminates the need for trust.

➢ Digital identification (ShoCard):

Identity theft and data security are two of the most pressing problems of our day. Many developed-world countries are working on compiling a centralized database of digital information on their people, which raises the specter of misuse of our personal information. Blockchain technology provides a possible answer by encrypting your key data in a block that can be confirmed by the blockchain network anytime you need to verify your identity. Passports and I.D. Cards are obvious replacements, but similar technology can also be used to replace passwords. If it's successful, it will be enormous.

There has long been suspicion that digital voting is both inaccurate and highly susceptible to manipulation, especially after Russia's involvement in the last

U.S election became public knowledge after the inquiry. To ensure voter privacy, blockchain technology verifies that a vote was correctly transmitted. In addition, because individuals will be able to vote using their mobile phones, this system promises to both decrease election fraud and boost overall voter participation.

Even while blockchain technology is relatively new, most of its potential uses are still a long way from being widely used. Blockchain platforms like Bitcoin, which have been around for a while, are prone to wild swings in price because of the technology's relative newness. Despite this, blockchain's potential to address some of the world's most pressing issues makes it a very alluring and compelling technology to follow. In any case, I'll keep a lookout for it.

In the past ten years, whether you've followed banking, investing, or cryptocurrencies, you've probably heard of "blockchain," the record-keeping system that powers the Bitcoin network. And it's possible that it only makes sense up to a point. A standard description of blockchain is "blockchain is a decentralized public ledger," which you've undoubtedly come across when researching the topic.

Blockchain isn't as complicated as its description suggests.

What does the term "blockchain" mean?

Why is it called "blockchain" if the technology is so complex? For the uninitiated, a blockchain is nothing more than a series of interconnected blocks. When we use the terms "block" and "chain," we mean digital information (the "block") that has been deposited in a public database.

The blockchain's "blocks" are built out of digital data. They are divided into three sections:*

Blocks keep track of transactions like the date, time, and dollar amount of your most recent Amazon purchase. This Amazon example is for demonstration purposes only; Amazon retail does not operate on the blockchain concept at the time of writing.

Blocks keep track of who is involved in a transaction. For example, your name and Amazon.com, Inc. would be recorded in a block for a large purchase from Amazon (AMZN). A unique "digital signature," which is similar to a username, is used to record your purchase instead of your real name.

The information that differentiates one block from another is stored in the form of blocks. A "hash" is a numerical number that identifies a particular block on the blockchain, just as you and I have names to identify one another. Some algorithms generate hashes, which are cryptographic codes. For example, let's suppose you bought a luxury item from Amazon, but when it's on the way, you realize you can't resist and need a second one as well. Your new transaction's information will be almost similar to your previous purchase, but the blocks may be distinguished by their unique codes.

To give you an idea of how things work, here's an example of a block being used to store a single Amazon purchase: The Bitcoin blockchain's block storage capacity is 1 MB each block. Therefore, the number of transactions that may fit inside a single block depends on the size of the transactions.

An Overview of How Blockchain Technology Works

A block is added to the blockchain when it contains new data. Blockchain is made up of a series of interconnected blocks. Four conditions must be met before a block may be added to the blockchain:

There must be a transaction. Let's stick with the hasty Amazon buy as an example. It's against your better judgment, yet you decide to buy something after rushing through the checkout process many times. A block, as previously mentioned, often contains possibly hundreds of transactions. Thus your Amazon purchase will be combined with the transaction details of other users.

It's important to double-check the transaction. Once you've made your purchase, you'll need to confirm the details of your transaction. A person is in charge of verifying new data entries in other public information records, such as the Securities and Exchange Commission, Wikipedia, or your local library. The blockchain, on the other hand, delegated this task to a distributed network of computers instead. Your transaction is verified by this vast network of computers as soon as you complete your Amazon purchase. So they check the purchase's specifics, such as when it happened, how much it cost, and who participated in it. I'll explain how this works in a moment.)

It is necessary to keep track of this transaction in a separate block. Your transaction will be approved after the accuracy has been confirmed. Your digital signature is stored in a block together with Amazon's digital signature. There, the transaction will most likely be one among hundreds or perhaps thousands.

A hash value must be assigned to that block. Once all of a block's transactions have been confirmed, it must be given a hash code to identify it uniquely. This is similar to giving wings to an angel. The hash of the most recent block added to the blockchain is likewise included in the block. The block may then be added to the blockchain once it has been hashed.

Upon adding a new block to the blockchain, it becomes accessible for everyone to see, including you. Take a look at the Bitcoin blockchain to see that you have access to transaction data and information on when, where, and who added the block to the blockchain ("Relayed By").

When it comes to privacy, does the blockchain meet your expectations?

Anybody may see the blockchain's contents, but users can also choose to join the blockchain network as nodes by connecting their computers. Whenever a new block of the blockchain is uploaded, their computer gets an automatic update, similar to how a Facebook News Feed provides a real-time update every time a new status is written.

This implies that there are hundreds, or even millions, of copies of the identical blockchain on every computer connected to the blockchain network. Even though each copy of the blockchain is identical, the information is more difficult to alter when distributed over a computer network. This is because blockchain eliminates the possibility of a single, distorted account of events. As an alternative, a hacker would have to alter every copy of the blockchain in the system. This is what is meant by a "distributed" ledger in the context of blockchain technology.

However, if you look at the Bitcoin blockchain, you'll see that you have no way of knowing who is making transactions. Personal information about individuals is restricted to their digital signature or username on the blockchain, even if transactions aren't entirely anonymous.

We must ask: how can we have faith in blockchain and its network if we have no way of knowing who is contributing blocks?

Is it safe to use blockchain?

There are many ways in which blockchain technology addresses security and trust concerns. In the first place, all new blocks are stored in a logical and chronological order as they arrive. To put it another way, they're always appended at the "very end" of the chain. A location on the chain is called a "height" assigned to each block in Bitcoin's blockchain. The tower's height has risen to 615,400 feet as of January 2020.

The block's content cannot be changed once it has been appended to the end of the blockchain. The reason for this is because each block includes a hash together with the previous block's hash. Using a math function, hash codes scramble digital data into a random string of numbers and characters. Thus, the hash code changes whenever the data is modified in any manner.

Why does it matter in terms of security? If a hacker succeeds in altering your Amazon transaction, they will have forced you to pay for your item twice. The block's hash will be updated as soon as the dollar value in your transaction is modified. Hackers would have to replace the old hash in the following block to hide their traces since it will be in the chain after them. The hash value of that block would be altered as a result. Then there's the next one, and the one after that.

A hacker would have to alter every subsequent block on the blockchain to alter a single one. If all those hashes were recalculated, it would require an astronomically large amount of computer power to do so. A new block on the blockchain can only be created, not edited, or deleted beyond that point.

Blockchain networks have added checks for computers that wish to join and contribute blocks to the chain to solve the trust mentioned above problem. In addition, a blockchain network requires members to "prove" themselves before they can join the tests, which are referred to as "consensus models." "Proof of work" is a typical illustration of how Bitcoin uses cryptography.

This method requires computers to "prove" their worth by resolving a mathematical issue that is difficult for them to comprehend on a computer. One of these issues must be solved before the computer may add a block to the blockchain. Adding blocks to the blockchain, often known as "mining," is a laborious operation. There was a 1 in 15.5 trillion chance of fixing one of these issues on the Bitcoin network in January 2020. 1 Computers must run programs that use a lot of power and energy to answer complex arithmetic problems under such conditions (read: money).

Hacker assaults are not rendered impossible by proof of work, but they are rendered less effective. For example, to organize a blockchain assault, a hacker would need to control more than 50% of the blockchain's computer power, which would overwhelm all other network members. Were it not for the enormous size of the Bitcoin blockchain, a so-called 51% assault would have been pointless.

Bitcoin vs. Blockchain

Blockchain aims to enable the recording and distribution of digital information but not the editing of such information. But, of course, it's hard to grasp the idea of blockchain technology without seeing it in action, so let's look at how the first implementation of this technology works.

Two academics, Stuart Haber and W. Scott Stornetta, originally proposed blockchain technology in 1991 to ensure the integrity of document time-stamps. However, blockchain did not have its first real-world use until almost two decades later, in January 2009, with the introduction of Bitcoin.

To use Bitcoin, you must use the blockchain protocol. Bitcoin's pseudonymous inventor Satoshi Nakamoto described it as "a revolutionary electronic cash system that is completely peer-to-peer, with no trusted third party" in an introductory research paper to the digital currency.

This is how it works. There are many individuals with bitcoin all around the globe. Many millions of individuals across the globe are likely to have some bitcoins in their possession. Think of it this way: one in a million bitcoin holders wants to buy groceries with their cryptocurrency. The blockchain comes into play here.

A central authority, typically a bank or government, regulates and verifies the usage of printed currency; Bitcoin, on the other hand, is entirely decentralized. Rather than relying on a central authority, a distributed network of computers verifies bitcoin transactions. "Decentralized" refers to the fact that a single entity does not control the Bitcoin network and blockchain.

When a user of the Bitcoin network sends money to another user in exchange for commodities, the computers in the network compete to verify the transaction. A "hash" is a challenging mathematical issue that users must attempt to solve using computer software. When a computer "hashes" a block to find a solution, it verifies the transactions in the block as well. To summarize, the completed transaction is saved in a blockchain block, making it impossible to change. Computers that correctly verify blocks on Bitcoin and most other blockchains are compensated with cryptocurrency. Mining is the term used to describe this activity.

Although blockchain transactions are available to everyone, user data is not or is not available as a whole. Therefore, an application known as a "wallet" is required for all transactions on the Bitcoin network. A public key and a private key are required for every wallet. Each key has a different cryptographic hash value. The public key serves as a repository and a withdrawal point for cryptocurrency transactions. Additionally, this key appears as the user's digital signature on the blockchain ledger itself.

There is no way for individuals to withdraw bitcoins that they have received through a payment to their public key. While the private key is long and complex enough, the short public key is generated using a simple mathematical formula. Unfortunately, the equation is so complicated that creating a private key from a public one is almost impossible. As a result, blockchain is regarded as a private technology.

Introduction to Public/Private Key Pairs

Here's the "Explain it Like I'm 5" version, abbreviated as ELI5 for short. A public key is like a school locker, and a private key is like the combination of that locker. Teachers, students, and even your crush may use the hole in your locker to leave notes and messages for you. However, the mailbox's contents can only be retrieved by a single individual with a unique key. Unlike school locker combinations maintained in the principal's office, the private keys to a blockchain network are not stored in a central database. In the instance of this guy, who made global news in December of 2017, if a user loses their private key, they will not access their bitcoin wallet.

A Single, Open Chain of Command

The blockchain is not only shared and maintained by a public network of users in the Bitcoin network, but it is also agreed upon. Whenever new blockchain blocks are uploaded, users' linked computers get an updated copy of the blockchain. Human mistake or hacker activity may result in one user's copy of the blockchain being modified such that it differs from all other copies.

A mechanism termed "consensus" is used by the blockchain protocol to discourage the creation of numerous blockchains. The consensus mechanism will use the longest chain if there are several divergent versions of the blockchain. As the number of people using a blockchain grows, new blocks may be added faster, increasing the chain's length. As a result, most users will always put their confidence in the blockchain of records. Blockchain technology's consensus mechanism is a strength, but it also provides for a vulnerability.

Hacker-Proof in theory

A hacker might theoretically use a 51 percent assault to take advantage of the majority rule. Here's how it'd go down in real life. If five million machines are connected to the Bitcoin network, it's a vast understatement, but it can be divided relatively easily. A hacker would need to control 2.5 million machines or more to get control of the network as a whole. An attacker, or group of attackers, might disrupt the process of registering new transactions if they were successful in doing so. Using this technique, they could transfer money and then reverse it, seeming to have more money than they had. Double-spending is a vulnerability that may allow users to spend their bitcoins more than once, making it the digital equivalent of a perfect counterfeit.

An assault of this magnitude would require gaining control of millions of computers, which is almost impossible on the Bitcoin network. When Bitcoin was initially launched in 2009, it would have been much simpler for a hacker to get control of the network's computing power due to the small number of users. It's been noted that one of the weaknesses of new cryptocurrencies is the decentralized nature of the blockchain.

The fear of 51 percent assaults among blockchain users may serve to prevent monopolies from developing. When a group of users known as "Bitfury" pooled thousands of powerful computers together to gain a competitive edge on the blockchain, journalist Nathaniel Popper wrote about it in his New York Times article, "Digital Gold: Bitcoin and the Inside Story of the Misfits and Millionaires Trying to Reinvent Money." They wanted to mine as many blocks as possible to earn as much bitcoin as possible, worth around $700 apiece at the time.

Using Bitfury to our Advantage

However, Bitfury has already surpassed 50% of the overall computing capacity of the blockchain network by March 2014. It chose self-regulation and promised never to exceed a 40% share of the network rather than expanding its control. A 51 percent assault would devalue bitcoin if people sold their coins ahead of time due to Bitfury's decision to keep gaining control over the network. Meaning that the information on blockchain network risks becoming useless if users lose confidence in it. When it comes to computing power, blockchain users can only go so far without losing money.

The Use of Blockchain in Real Life

We've established that blocks on the blockchain hold information about monetary transactions. However, it has been discovered that blockchain may also be used to store data regarding non-crypto currency transactions. For example, data regarding property transfers, supply chain breaks, and even votes for a candidate may be stored using blockchain technology.

A network of companies that provide professional services Regarding incorporating blockchain into their company processes, Deloitte recently evaluated 1,000 businesses in seven countries. According to their poll results, 34% of respondents already have a blockchain system in place, with a further 41% planning to do so within the following year. The study also revealed that almost 40% of the businesses questioned plan to spend $5 million or more on blockchain projects in the next year. Here are a few of the most well-known blockchain applications currently under investigation.

Use of a Bank

Banking is one of the industries that stands to gain the most from the use of blockchain technology. There are only five days a week when financial institutions are open for business, and those are only during regular business hours. You'll have to wait until Monday morning if you attempt to deposit a check on Friday at 6 p.m., for example. Even though you make your deposit within regular business hours, it may take up to three days for the transaction to be verified, owing to the high number of transactions banks must settle each day, whereas Blockchain is always on. As soon as a block is added to the blockchain, customers will complete their transactions in as little as 10 minutes. This is no matter what time of day or week it is. Banks will be able to trade money across institutions more swiftly and securely thanks to blockchain technology. For example, the settlement and clearing procedure in the stock trading industry may take up to three days (or more if banks trade abroad), meaning that money and shares are locked during that period.

Even if the money is just in transit for a few days, banks face substantial expenses and dangers because of the large amounts involved. A European bank, Santander, estimated annual savings of $20 billion. According to Capgemini, a French consulting firm, customers may save up to $16 billion annually in banking and insurance costs by using blockchain-based apps.

Incorporate into a Cryptographic Format

Cryptocurrencies like Bitcoin are built on top of blockchain technology. As previously discussed, a central authority, such as a bank or government, regulates and verifies currencies like the U.S. dollar. The data and money of a user are subject to the whims of their bank or government under the central authority system. The value of a user's money may be jeopardized if their bank fails or they reside in an area with an unstable government. These are the concerns that led to the creation of Bitcoin.

Bitcoin and other cryptocurrencies may function independently of a central authority thanks to the distributed ledger technology (blockchain) that distributes activities over a network of computers. As a result, there is less risk, and there are also fewer processing and transaction costs to pay. There are also more uses and a broader network of people and organizations in countries with unstable currencies, both domestically and internationally, for those who use it (at least, this is the goal.)

Uses in Health Care

Health care professionals may use blockchain to preserve patient medical data safely. For example, as soon as a medical record is created and signed, it may be added to the blockchain. This gives patients peace of mind knowing that the record can never be altered without their knowledge. In addition, these health data might be encoded with a private key and kept on the blockchain to ensure anonymity. This would limit access to only those who have the key.

Use of Real Estate Records

The procedure of registering property rights may be time-consuming and inefficient if you've ever visited your local Recorder's Office. An actual title deed must now be presented to a government employee at the county recording office. It will be manually recorded into the central county database and made available to the public for viewing. If there is a disagreement about property ownership, the parties involved must agree using the general index.

Not only does this procedure take a long time and money, but there is also much room for human mistakes, which makes it more challenging to trace down who owns what. The use of blockchain technology can remove the need for local recording offices to scan documents and hunt down physical files. Owners will have peace of mind knowing that their deed is correct and irrevocable if recorded and validated on the blockchain.

Use in Contracts with Smart Parties

A smart contract uses computer code embedded into the blockchain to facilitate, verify, or negotiate a contract agreement. Smart contracts work as long as everyone agrees to the terms. Then, if specific criteria are fulfilled, the agreement's provisions will be immediately implemented.

Let's say I use a smart contract to rent you my flat. As soon as you pay your security deposit, I'll give you the apartment's door code. The smart contract would keep onto my door code and immediately swap it for your security deposit on the day of the rental for both of us. The smart contract cancels and returns your security deposit as soon as the rental date passes without me sending you the door code. Using a notary or a third-party mediator usually comes with costs.

Utilization of a Distributed Manufacturing System

Suppliers may use blockchain to keep track of the provenance of the commodities they buy. In addition to health and ethical labels like "Organic," "Local," and "Fair Trade," this would enable businesses to verify the legitimacy of their goods.

In line with Forbes' reporting, the food sector is increasingly relying on blockchain to monitor the location and safety of food as it travels from the farm to the consumer.

Making use of it in the voting process

Election fraud may be eliminated, and voter participation increased with blockchain voting, as shown in the November 2018 midterm elections in West Virginia. Votes are recorded on the blockchain as blocks, making it virtually difficult to tamper with them after they've been cast. Transparency in the voting process is another benefit of blockchain technology since it saves time and money by eliminating poll workers.

Benefits and Drawbacks of Using Blockchain

Despite its intricacy, the potential of blockchain as a decentralized record-keeping system is almost limitless. Furthermore, blockchain technology may have uses beyond those listed above, such as improved user privacy and security, reduced processing costs, and reduced mistake rates.

Pros

- ❖ Greater precision due to the absence of human intervention in the verification process
- ❖ The elimination of third-party verification reduces costs.
- ❖ This makes it far more difficult to mess with
- ❖ Secure, confidential, and fast transactions
- ❖ Technology that is open and accessible

Cons

- ❖ The mining of bitcoin comes at a high expense in terms of technology.
- ❖ A small number of transactions take place per second
- ❖ Use in illegal actions in the past
- ❖ Vulnerability to hacking
- ❖ In greater depth, below are the benefits of blockchain for companies already on the market.
- ❖ Chain's precision

A network of hundreds of millions of computers approves transactions on the blockchain network. Consequently, there is less room for human mistakes, and the recorded information is more accurate as a result. Furthermore, even if a machine on the network committed a clerical error, it would only affect one copy of the blockchain. This is because it would need the mistake being made by at least 51% of the network's computers to propagate to the remainder of the blockchain, which is almost impossible.

Reduced Prices

To verify a transaction, a notary notarizes it, or a clergyman performs a marriage ceremony, customers often pay the bank or notary or priest. Through the use of blockchain, third-party verification is no longer required, along with the accompanying fees that go along with it. For example, when businesses accept credit card payments, they pay a modest charge to the bank since the transaction must be processed. Instead of a centralized authority, Bitcoin has no transaction fees and practically no transaction costs.

Decentralization

Because it doesn't have a central database, blockchain eliminates the need for centralized storage. Instead, a network of computers copies the blockchain. It is very uncommon for a whole network of computers to be updated whenever a new block of data is included in the blockchain Blockchain makes it more difficult to tamper with information by dispersing it over a network rather than keeping it in a single database. If a hacker managed to get his hands on a copy of the blockchain, just a single copy of the data would be compromised rather than the whole network.

Transactions that are Quick and Easy

The settlement of transactions made via a central authority may take many days. The money may not appear in your account until Monday morning if you deposit a check Friday evening. Whereas banks are only open during regular business hours, five days a week, the blockchain is open 24/7. After just a few hours, transactions are deemed secure and may be executed in as little as 10 minutes. This is especially helpful for cross-border transactions due to the time zone differences and the need for all parties to approve payment processing before a deal can be finalized.

Transactions That Are Not Public

As a result, many blockchain networks function as open databases that anybody with an internet connection may access. Even while consumers have access to transaction data, they do not have any way of knowing who made the transactions. It's a widespread misconception that decentralized ledger technologies like bitcoin's blockchain are anonymous; in reality, they're just private.

As a result, when a user conducts a public transaction, their public key code, rather than personal information, is stored on the blockchain. Of course, it's still possible for hackers to get a user's personal information if a bank is compromised, but that's not the case with blockchain.

Completely Secure transactions

The blockchain network must verify the validity of a transaction once it has been recorded. Numerous computers on the blockchain race to verify the transaction's accuracy, resulting in a deluge of confirmations. A block is created on the blockchain after a computer has verified the transaction. On the blockchain, each block has its unique hash and the previous block's unique hash. A block's hash code changes when the information on it is modified in any manner, but the hash code on the block following it does not. Due to this disparity, it's almost impossible to change the blockchain's data without anybody knowing about it first.

Transparency

Aside from personal information being kept private, much of the blockchain technology is available as open source. As long as most of the network's computing power backs a given change, blockchain network members have complete freedom to alter the code. Since the blockchain is open-source, it is far more difficult for someone to tamper with the data. Anyone who tries to modify the blockchain network will be caught since millions of machines are connected at all times.

The drawbacks of using blockchain

The blockchain has many advantages, but it also faces many obstacles on the way to widespread use. Today, there are a variety of challenges standing in the way of the widespread use of blockchain technology. To incorporate blockchain into existing business networks, hundreds of hours (read: money) of bespoke software design and back-end programming are needed. These are political and legislative obstacles primarily. Here are a few roadblocks to the broad adoption of the blockchain.

The price of the new technology

Although blockchain may save customers money by eliminating transaction fees, it is an extremely expensive piece of software to learn and use. Bitcoin employs a "proof of work" mechanism that requires enormous computing power to validate transactions. The electricity used by the bitcoin network's millions of machines is comparable to Denmark's yearly consumption in the real world. In addition, a recent analysis by the research firm Elite Fixtures found that the cost of mining a single bitcoin varies dramatically depending on where you are, from as little as $531 to a mind-boggling $26,170.

The actual cost is more like $4,758 if you use typical US utility prices. Despite the high expense of mining bitcoin, many people continue to utilize energy to verify blockchain transactions. When bitcoin miners contribute a new block to the blockchain, they are rewarded with bitcoin. To verify transactions on non-crypto currency blockchains, miners will need to be compensated or otherwise motivated.

Ineffectiveness in terms of speed

The potential inefficiencies of the blockchain may best be shown by looking at Bitcoin. To add a new block to the blockchain, Bitcoin's "proof of work" mechanism has to be run for approximately 10 minutes. According to current estimates, the blockchain network can handle no more than seven transactions per second at this pace (TPS). Thus, Bitcoin is still constrained by the blockchain, even though competing cryptocurrencies like Ethereum (20 TPS) and Bitcoin Cash (60 TPS) perform better. To put things in perspective, Visa's legacy brand can handle 24,000 TPS.

Contravention of the Law

While the blockchain network's secrecy protects users from attacks and safeguards their privacy, it also allows for illicit trade and other blockchain network activities. Silk Road, an online "dark web" bazaar that operated from February 2011 until October 2013 when the FBI shut it down, is perhaps the most recognized example of blockchain being used for illegal activities.

Users were able to browse the website anonymously and make unauthorized bitcoin purchases. However, users of online exchanges like blockchain-based ones cannot enjoy complete anonymity due to current U.S. regulations. For example, customers in the United States must provide information about themselves when opening an account with an online exchange. In addition, each client's identification must be verified, and the fact that the consumer does not appear on any list of known or suspected terrorist groups.

Anxiety at the US Federal Reserve

The Federal Reserve, the Bank of Canada, and the Bank of England are among the central banks looking at digital currencies. However, Bank of England researchers said in a Feb. 2015 study paper that further research is needed to develop a system that uses distributed ledger technology without jeopardizing a central bank's capacity to manage its currency and protect the system against systemic assault.

Permeability to a Hack

A 51% assault is more likely to target newer coins and blockchain networks. The computing power needed to acquire majority control of a blockchain network makes these assaults very difficult to carry out. Still, NYU computer science researcher Joseph Bonneau believes that may change in the future. As hackers may now rent computing capacity rather than purchase all of the equipment, Bonneau published a study last year predicting that 51% of assaults will rise.

Is There Anything More to Come for the Blockchain?

Blockchain, a technology that was first suggested as a research project in 1991, is now in its late twenties. Nevertheless, like other millennials of its generation, blockchain has been the subject of considerable public interest in the past two decades, with companies across the globe speculating on the potential of the technology and its future direction.

In part because of bitcoin and other cryptocurrencies, blockchain has finally made a name for itself at the age of twenty-seven with many practical applications already deployed and researched. In addition, blockchain is a hot topic among investors because of its potential to improve the accuracy, efficiency, and security of corporate and government processes.

As we enter the third decade of blockchain, the issue is no longer "if" but "when" traditional businesses will adopt the technology.

CHAPTER FIVE

WHAT IS THE AGILE METHOD?

With dexterous jobs, the executives mainly portray an accumulation of advanced methods for software, which are now more than a decade old and are becoming ubiquitous with many associations, both big and little, and not just limited to the product industry. They have also been developed. When organizations adopt Agile methods, they can better enhance the quality of their products and services while also ensuring that these products and services can be brought to market quickly and competently.

Since Agile has such high levels of efficiency, it is usual to observe a marked increase in a company's growth and overall expansion when it begins using across-the-board Agile methods to manage its endeavors. By elevating and responding to change naturally, the board strategy allows the company to cope with venture development flexibly. This methodology differs from traditional methods. The task's outcome is predetermined and cannot be changed, but this does not mean that the board of Agile ventures has a haphazard approach to undertakings.

In comparison to older methods, Agile's result is consistently less unexpected, but this isn't a barrier to the project's progress. On the contrary, it is more productive to choose a strategy that reacts positively when faced with change, resolving problems as they arise, than to adopt a strategy that moves ahead indiscriminately towards its final goal, never seeming to consider a change of direction.

By giving partners who take personal responsibility for the project's outcome the freedom to collaborate effectively, the board enables them to achieve their goals. Therefore, it is critical to have regular group meetings to collaborate and keep everyone on task and productive. The group may be brought up to speed on the latest progress at these first get-togethers before establishing plans for the next part of the process and preparing for its conclusion. As a result of their shared skills and abilities, colleagues may successfully finish projects by assigning each task to the most reasonable colleague.

Working on Agile projects means that all groups involved should be located under the same roof (i.e., one office), allowing workers to form more solid relationships and provide unquestionably more space. However, this isn't a pressing matter. Because of the amazing display of innovation we have at our disposal to assist communication, it is extremely straightforward to use Agile principles successfully in a wide range of distinct situations. Nevertheless, this economy's present state hints at a significant challenge, emphasizing successful execution.

The CEOs' deft undertaking brings a lot to the table. Agile venture the board encourages organizations to compete and remain abreast of the pace in a rapidly changing, diverse global market via its ground-breaking strategy that focuses on collaboration and coordinated effort. If rationality and flexibility are important considerations for you, Agile is a superior option to traditional approaches and should be thoroughly investigated as a viable alternative.

These methods are used to create highly flexible programming programs that are both isolated and hearty and are thus known as Lithe Development procedures. One of the most common misconceptions regarding the agile process is that it has no prerequisites for nimble participation in the board. Furthermore, a small number of individuals notice that joint projects continue to operate even when no one else is there. This insight is often brought about by the lack of attention paid to the finer details. It impacts relocating a venture director from one area to another since the association discourages supervising people.

The success or failure of any project is determined by the degree of adherence to tasks that the executives form from the time of planning to the time of handover of the project. If the board does not make the necessary investments, a task may go for a hurl and miss the deadlines, becoming a burden and increasing the cost. Using verified information and re-designed segments, the process of setting up the board advances quickly thanks to major advancements in programming that closely follow the techniques of setting up the board's executives.

Different Agile Project Management middle-of-the-road methods are employed:

The item merchant, whose movement focuses on dealing with the task's vision, owns the endeavor. First, the item merchant may create, progress, and deliver the item form as necessary. Next, the item owner begins obtaining funding for the venture by developing an initial discharge strategy and collecting the most basic assets.

The item merchant is in charge of handling the ROI activity (Return on Investment). Additionally, the item owner is in charge of several responsibilities, such as monitoring the venture's ROI goals and speculative vision. In the same way, the seller of the item offers to replenish the stock and arrange to ensure that highly regarded utility is produced first and foremost. Despite this, the item's seller weighs success against the associated expenses.

In the company, a person in charge of forwarding progress is in charge. In this cycle, the project leader creates the team and identifies the highest priority needs compared to the overall accumulation of items. Along with each other, they make each task on a dash build-up much more apparent, and they win when it comes to completing assigned tasks.

Method 1: Scrum

The Scrum Master takes responsibility for progress by ensuring that the project and the organizational culture are enhanced to reach the project's ROI goals under the Scrum process.

Method 2: XP

It is a product enhancement approach to enhance the nature of programming and increase responsiveness to customers' changing requirements. Extraordinary Programming. Encouraging frequent releases in short development cycles as a portion of deft programming improvement empowers improved profitability and introduces checking points where new customer requirements may be acquired. It's a sure bet since it's built on customer loyalty. There are five important ways to develop a product venture - communication is one of them.

Method 3: The Waterfall

When it comes to software development, the Waterfall method is a step-by-step structural process. Assembling and developing parts is where it gets its start in the world's standard work process system. When it comes to software enhancement, venture capitalists use two methods: Lithe and Waterfall. Both have their unique strengths and flaws. Numerous venture-driven components influence the choice of these methods. The benefit of the Waterfall method is that it divides the project into smaller, more manageable pieces, which reduces the reliance on humans.

If you're a Team Leader or Project Manager at a company, you've probably heard of the Agile methodology. This topic has generated a great deal of discussion, and some remarkable individuals believe we must deal with two opposing concepts: the horrible Agile and the wonderful Agile.

The wonderful thing about Agile is that it's the management style you should use every time you're dealing with programming improvement. It's simple: use good tracking software like Track (which is free) or FogBugz (expensive). The two tools are unique; they bear no resemblance to Microsoft Project at all. You're under no obligation to use Gants unless you've been asked to do so. If a task has the potential to become a pundit, it should be prioritized, and the designer should get to work on it right away.

You can use a combination of bugs and highlights, just like you would in reality, and you can use advanced highlights like time following to make a mix of highlights and bugs. Trying to keep up with a graph is an agony that every old school administrator remembers well, but it's not practical. Likewise, working in a closed unapproved organization will be a living nightmare to monitor project updates and cutoff deadlines.

As a manager, your dynamic role is similar to that of a love seat: you try to assist the group leaders and the group by resolving fundamental problems that arise when a project is in progress. Don't be afraid to look at the code and learn from the designers adjacent to each other. Your project's diagram won't be as good if you stay too far away from the code.

You've taken a shot at something new, and it worked well, but you couldn't figure out why. When we first started using Agile, we achieved a great deal. With a bespoke CRM implementation that had previously gone wrong, we were able to turn it around into a major win for a major insurance company. But, even though the executives' apparatus is doing an amazing job, many people still don't know much about Agile and how it works. So, here's a quick visual representation of what Agile Project Management does for your business.

The Agile Manifesto was signed in 2001, and the phrase "Lithe Software Advancement" was coined. Some of the world's most eminent figures gathered at this landmark event to energize themselves against the "heavyweight" momentum improvement methods of the time (also known as a cascade). From that point on, Agile gained popularity as a natural method of self-improvement. In today's world, the use of Agile methodologies is spreading rapidly, with organizations like the Project Management Institute starting to take notice.

Extreme Programming, Lean, Scrum, and other methods are all included under the name Agile. In light of the most current data available in the industry, Scrum has a 49.1 percent stake (Version One "The State of Agile Development" third Annual Survey: 2008). All Agile processes have the following characteristics, although each system has its own unique set of contrasts.

- ❖ Start by creating the most impressive value indicators.
- ❖ Visit discharges and short cycles
- ❖ The scope of the project remains flexible despite the presence of fixed assets and time.
- ❖ High permeability and data transmission synchronization (otherwise known as eye to eye)
- ❖ Small, self-managing groups with a variety of purposes
- ❖ Inspection and rectification (persistent improvement)

Project Management solutions have evolved to provide excellent results and reduce the start-to-finish conveyance cycle when adaptability and flexibility are current expressions, and conventional is obsolete. Agile (or Extreme) Project Management is slowly but surely making inroads to dislodge the Project Management discipline from its deeply procedure-driven approach (as established by PMI and APMG in their particular PMP and PRINCE2 models).

Project management aims to bring about beneficial change or enhance the value of achieving certain objectives and goals, and this is crucial to the success of a project's completion.

A Critical Success Factor (CSF) takes form due to efficient correspondence as the lattice connections grow. It's critical to have connections between clients and frameworks if you want to achieve your objective. Light-footed aids in strengthening how communication among all those involved in independent endeavor forms 'THE Key.' Correspondence will no longer be restricted to important stakeholders. Voila!

Another way to measure is to estimate the amount of time it will take to complete a project. Agile helps accomplish that by removing required archives from the project and replacing them with new customer stories.

On the other hand, the Customer is the most critical component of this kind of executive arrangement. Customers' requirements may diverge with time, especially in such a dynamic industry as today's. Spry ensures that this objective is met by allowing clients to make changes to their requests throughout the way. It goes a long way toward giving the customer peace of mind.

It is a result-oriented project management system, like Nimble.

Unlike the traditional model that relies on a strict consecutive approach, the new model concludes design before each errand is executed.

In contrast to the traditional method, which involves creating unit test plans later or while developing, this approach begins with creating the unit test plans upfront.

The masterstroke of Agile is the criticism well-disposed state instead of relying on conventional gadgets and techniques where it surpasses previous Project the board system. This new way of working stands out since it incorporates a feeling of openness among all parties involved, especially the venture group. Each step concludes with a tried-and-true final product that earns customer approval as sign-offs, energizing the team to do even more in the future.

There are many phrase progressions in Agile Scrum Methodology as well. For example, Scrum Master replaces Venture Manager, and Product Owner replaces Project Sponsor/Customer. Therefore, venture Manager and Scrum Master are no longer needed. Likewise, it's very uncommon to hear people refer to animals using vivified words such as "Sprint," "Chicken," and "Pig."

Philosophy appropriation has become more important at business meetings as Agile's adoption spreads. What's true is that you may use whatever fits your needs best, and you're not restricted to using just one kind or combining several types.

Web-Based Project Management systems must be properly constructed in today's competitive corporate environments, or a specialized hand should be encouraged to dominate. For businesses to perform better and address key issues, Bizixx Business Agreements is a leading Online Project Management System solution.

The PMBOK or PRINCE in general, or portions of it, continue to be battled by organizations worldwide, ensuring that they are excessively confusing, involved and detract from the time required to develop project expectancies. APF is the hero because it adapts to the constantly changing business circumstances.

For clients, APF is a technique that iterates and adapts to meet their time and cost constraints while maintaining a consistent factor degree at each point of focus. Towards the conclusion of each focus, the customer has the opportunity to modify the direction of the endeavor based on what was learned from each previous cycle, comprehending and supervising change rather than avoiding it.

Five phases define agile project framework:

- ❖ Scope of the Version
- ❖ Determine what is needed and what will be done to solve the problem by creating Conditions Of Satisfaction (COS).
- ❖ The issue/opportunity, what will be done and how it will be done, the financial value of the venture, as well as potential pitfalls, assumptions, and roadblocks to advancement
- ❖ Functional requirements should take precedence; this list is subject to change, but it currently reflects the best available information.
- ❖ Create a mid-level Work Breakdown Structure that demonstrates specific, important competencies and sub-capabilities.

Focus on the three-pointed scope triangle (comprising of time, cost, assets, extension, and quality, consumer loyalty was forgotten about)

- ❖ Plan your journey with a cycle (iterative)
- ❖ Remove from the Work Breakdown Structure (WBS) the exercises that define the cycle's effectiveness.
- ❖ Break down the WBS into smaller, more manageable chunks.
- ❖ Create the circumstances for these initiatives to succeed.
- ❖ Disperse tasks across large groups and distribute teams to each group.

As part of the built-up cycle sequence of events and expenditure restrictions, each group develops a smaller scale level schedule with asset distributions for completion of their endeavors

- ❖ Build in a loop (iterative)
- ❖ Implement step-by-step planning to generate the value assigned to this cycle.
- ❖ Get the cycle work started.

❖ Keep track of and make adjustments to the cycle construction

When this cycle's time is over, it will come to an end. During the next cycle, any usefulness that was not completed during the current cycle is reevaluated as a significant part of its usefulness.

For any requests for changes and ideas on improvements, create an Upgrade Scope Bank.

❖ Create a Problems Log to keep track of all problems and progress toward their objectives.

❖ Checkpoint for the customer (iterative)

Clients play out a quality audit of usefulness produced in a recently completed cycle against a general goal of most extreme business value. Changes are made to the enhanced level arrangement and subsequent cycle work if required.

Rehashing the arrangement until the time and cost expenditure plans for this variation have been utilized - Cycle Plan/Cycle Build/Client Checkpoint

❖ Retrospective Evaluation Following the Release

❖ Check to see whether the expected business outcome was achieved

❖ Identify the findings that may be used to enhance the current setup.

Decide what can be done with the information gathered to make agile project frameworks more viable.

An overview of the Agile Method

Are you familiar with the term "agile" and how it works?

When using Deft, tasks are split into smaller units called "sprints." Each sprint is completed in a distinct period, usually between one and three weeks.

The customer (the undertaking owner) has some freedom since once each run is completed, a complete assessment of the work done to date is conducted. This gives the company owner a chance to see the product in action in the middle of the project. It is significant because it enables customers to see the beginning of the product in real life, which constantly generates constructive feedback and alterations to the scope. This is important

All requirements are reorganized for the next sprint once the product audit is completed. There is no connection with the engineers after the dash has started. Therefore the audit and re-prioritization will repeatedly occur until the job is completed. Ultimately.

When it comes to doing large programming projects, how can Agile help?

It's true that most customers already have a good idea of what they want, but it's almost impossible to think through every need before starting a new endeavor. The product engineers would depart and finish the project based on the record using standard programming enhancement methods, providing their customer a completed job at the end. Clients are less satisfied as a result since it's tough to take everything into account. In other words, the customer wanted X, but he only needed 20% of it since that's how much he needed.

With Agile, you're getting closer to your project's "true extension." The ability to get started more quickly

It's also a benefit of the Agile approach because you don't need to know all the specifics of your requirements to get started. This task can be measured with little more than a visual cue (give you a cost in addition to a spending plan). When you're working on a project, it's dynamic; if you decide you need one part, you may have to give up another, a less important one, to complete it on time and within budget.

It begins by admitting that the traditional "cascade" method of programming development is woefully inadequate in today's world. The "design, structure, create, test, convey" method works well when building cars or buildings, but it fails miserably when creating programming frameworks... Moreover, equipment, demand, and competition change rapidly in the corporate world, so savvy workers must walk the fine line between too much process and not enough.

Methodology Overview for the Spry Software Program

It eliminates the risk of spending months or years on a treatment that ultimately fails due to a little error made early on. Instead, trusting agents and organizations to work legally with clients to understand the goals and make agreements quickly and gradually is key.

1. Fast, yet smaller

Traditionally, progress in programming has relied on phases such as defining requirements, planning, constructing, testing, and distribution. Yet, paradoxically, the light-footed method aims to provide the main addition in half a month and the whole piece of programming in many months.

2. The ability to communicate

At every stage of the endeavor, smart business groups work together day in and day out in intimate and personal meetings. With this concerted effort and communication, even if circumstances alter, the process will stay on course.

3. Reactions

Instead of waiting until the delivery stage to see whether the goal was met, Agile teams regularly measure the goal's progress and pace. Then, after each addition is sent, the speed is calculated.

4. Trust

Have faith in the ability of Spry teams and employees to self-organize. Instead of waiting for the board to issue a declaration of standards to achieve the desired result, they understand the goals and find their method to contact them. Keep It Simple (KIS) is a guideline that members should follow when adjusting and modifying the process over time.

Agile methodologies have their own unique set of principles.

Some of the most popular methods for fusing Agile standards are as follows:

Iterative Development:

Iterative development is based on the principle of breaking a large project into smaller, manageable chunks called 'runs.'

Each team member has a specific task to complete throughout these runs, which may last two months. Daily meetings called standups, and a few graphical delineations like the 'burn to the ground' diagram keep the whole team up to date on the progress. In addition, a list is maintained where all tasks are documented and organized according to the requirements that customers or their middlemen either specify.

To ensure coherence, the Kanban method relies heavily on Kanban. The whole project is planned out on a process board, where the errands to be performed, the tasks to be completed, and the completed tasks are all noted separately. Compared to many other management theories, Kanban is simple to implement in an authoritative context where the official priority chain is considered.

The development of lean programming:

The focus of this approach is on enhancing the development of substantial value throughout the whole structure. It eliminates waste in the framework, such as fragmented work and the exchange of assignments. It prevents work from piling up and implies that additional work should be brought in to be completed successfully

XP:

Small groups use extraordinary programming or XP for small to medium-sized item improvement, especially when the requirements of the products are rapidly changing.

Precious stone:

This Agile approach provides advancement groups greater freedom and encourages them to develop the product and deal with problems independently. Procedures and equipment are valued less than people and their collaboration.

System Development Methodology for Dynamic Environments

It's used for projects with a limited budget and deadline. Additionally, this method focuses on supporting components such as the venture's feasibility, conducting a business analysis, developing a functional model, and finalizing the project's deliverables.

Driven Development is a Development Methodology.

FDD focuses on dividing the venture into little, customer-valued capabilities that may be delivered in a short period. As a result, individuals and their relationships are given much important value, and item development is seen as a human movement rather than a purely mechanical effort.

Rules for using the Agile Method in Project Management in the most effective manner

The following rules serve as the foundation for this strategy:

It is increasingly important to have working programming that records (must discharge new forms of programming at visit interims, and you need to keep the code simple and propelled, reducing documentation to a base); We must work together (so the improvement group ought to be permitted to recommend changes to the undertaking whenever).

A small number of papers exist inside this system, and they are mostly dependent on the organization's and venture administrator's needs and attitude. Any decision must consider the benefits and results of each kind of training before making a choice. The close involvement of customers in the development and configuration process compensates for the complete lack of structure or documentation, as in Extreme Programming.

This may be done via computerization if the goal is to focus only on programming processes and not participate in the side activities. This is preferable since doing so can cause many issues when programming improvement is made and may even alter the task's outcomes.

CHAPTER SIX

THE BASIC PRINCIPLES OF AGILE PROJECT MANAGEMENT AND HOW TO APPLY THEM

The product development business is very sensitive because of the high risk of competition. To cope with new programming and applications, the product industry employs a variety of distinct philosophical approaches. As a tool for venture executives in programming companies, Nimble Methodology is widely used. It is dependent on a process of continuous improvement. The method incorporates involvement from several association cross-practice groups to gather the required assets and answers for developing the best programming and applications. Using a lean method has the advantage of allowing for continual development throughout the progression process. Rather than simply achieving agreement satisfaction, the goal of a clever system is to win the complete allegiance of the customer. Using these methods also helps to keep the cost of programming enhancement to a minimum.

The fundamentals of shrewd venture planning

As a guide, these are the philosophical requirements for shrewd business people across the board:

1 - There's Hierarchy.

In the development group, the decision about whether to create a progressive structure depends heavily on the project manager's methodology; however, there's another outcome that's less clear: If your requirements call for an extremely large number of software engineers to work on different parts of your project simultaneously, you'll have the opportunity to do so if you insist on a divided tree structure.

2 - *Programming In Pairs.*

While one of the software engineers composes and the other executes while they both choose the ideal development arrangement while programming two by two (i.e., two developers), a workspace, a PC, and a console and mouse are all needed. However, there are helpful models which demonstrate how some software engineers may be awful and unproductive with this training; it is well known that it reduces the costs of the job.

3 - *Refactoring.*

A better result may be deduced from the completed changes to code that remain unchanged and from the outside look, the header language structure, and other little details. There are several well-known techniques in the management of programming projects that use this technique.

4 - *Enhancement of information is a priority.*

Established with the advent of Object-Oriented Programming is simply the acknowledgment of learning generation done in an organization as it creates code; this information produced must not be wasted and should be utilized to create new programming in the future.

5 - *Establish a close line of communication.*

The nodal lightweight method is made possible by Alistair Cockburn's viewpoint, who is considered by many to be the first scholar of lightweight processes. When we say we communicate directly, we correspond relationally with all of our business partners, including the client. To conduct an adequate needs assessment and to manage an effective software engineering activity even in the absence of any documentation.

6 - *The link with the client.*

Even though Extreme Programming is a complete integration that includes everyone, even the client, even the client takes an interest in weekly gatherings of software engineers. In addition, there are other cases where a client is only involved for a short period and then leaves, and still other cases where a client participates in a roundabout way and is used in the trial of a discharged employee. Thus, the customer's involvement can take many different forms.

7 - The Process Of Conceptualizing And Documenting.

This is a mistake: task managers should consider making archives rather than thinking that lightweight processes would eliminate the documentation and the plan altogether. Most project managers decide on the amount and kind of records needed to complete the product venture before further work on them.

Transports that are used regularly

It gives the customer "something to work with" and prevents delays in the complete structure's delivery by guaranteeing that they receive the item (programming) on time by making constant arrivals between time adjustments. This allows venture directors to achieve greater results on both sides at once. An undertaking director may obtain more precise information on customer requirements via this process. They would not be able to articulate without first seeing a working prototype of the product, which helps them see its flaws and shortcomings.

It all started with a sincere need for respect in "partner associations" over procedures and instruments. Agile advancement methodologies originated from a responsive programming change over thorough documentation and specialized coordinated effort over agreement arrangement over the smallest plans and timetables.

To put it another way, forms, gadgets, unnecessary paperwork, lengthy agreement exchanges, and a heavy dependence on organizing did not quickly or reliably provide a framework, capacity, and ability value. "Dexterous Development" was therefore created over 13 years and is still under development today.

When it comes to growth, Light-"esteem footed's focused approach" promotes fresh avenues for change and risk-taking on the board. New frameworks, capabilities, and ability esteem are emerging as custom-fit light-footed abilities and experiences increase in industry and government. However, there are risks when products and services are rushed into production without the necessary knowledge and diligence to anticipate problems before, during, and after delivery. The Agile approach is not a magic wand by any stretch of the imagination.

The ten most common Agile Development Principles:

Enhancing the partnership in light of conditions and dangers for executives

1) Collaborating with a partner and coordinating efforts

2) Specific criteria for a single point of authority and a large number of people participating in the event

3) Encouraging the use of tools that coordinate their efforts

4) The use of a predetermined chance and hazard-aware basic strategy

5) Regularly creating higher-level preconditions

6) Visual documentation that emphasizes "keep things simple."

7) Visit transport of streamlined capabilities and highlights

8) Conduct early and frequent tests

9) Lessons Learned brief coordination will become increasingly deft.

Spry is an umbrella term for a wide range of methodologies. One of the most comprehensive light-footed methodologies is called DSDM, or Dynamic Systems Development Methodology. It's a method of advancing programming that's slow, methodical, and collaborative. When using the DSDM method, you can keep an eye on project costs, quality, and schedule by defining extensions as indisputable criteria, such as "should haves" and "could haves."

There are two more manageable methodologies: Scrum and XP. "A flexible, all-encompassing item advancement procedure where an improvement group works as a unit to reach a common goal" is at the heart of the Scrum methodology. Using Scrum, venture partners and expertise controls are encouraged to self-organize, either physically or through a compelling online coordinated effort and daily face-to-face communication. Scrum's fundamental concept is that a project may change its view on what it needs and needs as the project advances; this specific approach enables quick delivery of new requirements. Another well-known dexterous programming advancement technique is Extraordinary Programming (XP), based on predefined programming design processes and is decided and produced accordingly.

Standard 1: Maintain customer loyalty by delivering content regularly

The work of programming isn't done to create software. As a result, an end-user may more easily do previously difficult or time-consuming tasks, resolve a problem, or execute their duties more effectively in general. The most important need for programming advancement, on the other hand, is frequently overlooked. Given the current situation, how could you possibly align yourself with this rule?

Less alteration arranged at once reduces the distance between requirements social event and customer critique. So you'll have a better chance of guiding the product in the right direction for your customers.

Standard 2: Don't be afraid to try new things.

You don't have to wait for the next framework to be put together or for a framework redesign before making modifications. Lithe processes deal with the client's advantage of change.

Reduce the time it takes to imagine and put into action major changes. Furthermore, even though it's late in the improvement process, don't hesitate to go forward.

Standard 3: Provide functional programming, with a preference for shorter delivery times.

In the past, advancement tactics were front-loaded with voluminous paperwork to provide the impression that all requirements for a particular project had been met. However, the usual result was little more than a mountain of paperwork with nothing to show for it when the project came to a close.

The board's dexterous endeavor revolves around reducing the distance between the areas of arrangement and transportation. As a result, the lean approach focuses more on creating programming than preparing for it. This allows you to enhance your work's quality and viability.

Standard 4: Developers and executives must work together

This one is critical, even though many individuals have difficulty putting it into practice. Executives and engineers working together is usually the best strategy for handling this. You may also make use of specialist telecommuter equipment. It makes it easier for people on opposite sides to see one another, which leads to more productive work.

Standard 5: Construction extends to include those who are motivated by it.

In dexterous undertaking the board, there should be no micromanagement. Collectively, we should behave in a naturally coordinated and autonomous manner. If feasible, assemble a crew you can rely on to complete the project's goals and provide the assistance and conditions needed to do business effectively.

Standard 6: Face-to-face collaboration is the most efficient and effective form of communication.

That said, the time elapsed between asking a question and receiving a response must be reduced. This is another reason why co-area or remote work is critical in light-footed tackling the board during those hours. When people work together under the same (virtual) roof, it's much easier to ask questions, offer suggestions, and communicate.

Standard 7: The working programming standard states that progress is dependent on it.

The following key metric should judge a nimble advancement group: The product isn't functioning as it should, right? If this isn't the case, then it doesn't matter how many words were written, problems were solved, or hours spent, etc. Every other step is unnecessary if you cannot succeed since a good group must provide excellent programming.

Standard 8: Agile processes promote the advancement of practical improvement

When working on a similar project for an EXTREMELY long period, burnout may be a common problem among dexterous development teams. Because excessive extra time cannot continue without compromising the quality, work should be done in brief lucrative bursts to avoid this. Pay attention to how fast your coworkers are moving so you can choose the right speed for you. Best practices typically dictate that employees be allowed to leave the office exhausted yet satisfied.

Standard 9: Constant evaluation of specialized excellence and significant plan improvements spryness

Engineers shouldn't hang on to unneeded or confusing code once it's been cleaned up. Instead, every iteration of the code should indicate progress. The product development team should employ scrum equipment and put aside an effort to assess their response along with a light-footed method. Cleaning up code "later" - which may equally mean never - is much more time-consuming than doing it while the project is still underway.

Standard 10: Keep things as simple as possible.

Limit the time between perception and completion and keep things simple. Stay away from the "bustling work" prevalent in corporate culture and doesn't make a difference. Use tools like Mashable, Trello, and InVision to keep track of your team and the hours they've put in.

Standard 11: The most effective frameworks, preconditions, and strategies overcome your tendency to associate with others who think like you

A nimble supervisory team gets its bearings on its own. People don't need to be told what to do; instead, they attack problems, deal with obstacles, and come up with solutions. If the project manager feels the need to micromanage, it should serve as a caution.

Standard 12: Examine and Correct

This is a crucial rule for CEOs who have a lean workload. First, the group should use regular intervals to consider ways to become more strong, tune and modify their behavior in the same way they do. Then, if there is a better way to move a project forward, the team should put it into action.

CHAPTER SEVEN

LEAN PRODUCT DEVELOPMENT

What is Lean?

Lean refers to any process change that has the net result of increasing your framework's throughput while also being more cost-effective.

This description helps us focus on equipment development and find ways to increase throughput in these systems while remaining fiscally sound significant.

Where can I learn about Lean Product Development?

Item advancement teams are in charge of coming up with new products that benefit their customers. Because of the vastness of this area's distinction between development and delivery (and thus value), this is a mysterious place to operate. For example, criticism of designing a particular component will not be received until the item is manufactured and in the client's hands. To put it another way, many decisions about structure and improvement will be made repeatedly based on short-cycle experiments and models. During the development process, emphasis is placed on creating reusable data and reducing risk at handoff points.

Whenever we discuss "Lean Product Development," we're looking at how we identify "Lean" logic and concepts throughout the item progression process. Despite many methods and tools, lean thinking calls for us to use a social environment. Therefore, key norms and practices are included, resulting in a state of constant progress. To proceed with a true Lean framework, both the method and the way of life structured by Lean practice must be accessible.

LPD, or Lean Product Development, employs Lean principles to solve Product Development's evolving challenges. Lean item advancement, which began with Allen Ward's research of the Toyota Production System, aims to solve the following issues explicitly:

- ❖ Shortening the time required for the progression process
- ❖ lowering the high costs of progressing
- ❖ The need for ever-more-creative solutions

Decreased generation costs.

Cycles of redevelopment

From where does Lean item improvement begin?

The Toyota Production System (TPS) is where Lean began, focusing on customer requirements (client esteem), pulling (undertakings) rather than pushing (errands), and making work visible to the group via Oobeya rooms. It also reduces risks and speeds up learning in Toyota's Product Development System (TPDS). TPS resulted in superior products that were delivered even faster and more reliably.

What's the difference between lean and agile methods of item advancement?

Many of the guiding principles of Lean are found in coordinated improvement. For example, client requirements and learning (iterative improvement) are at its heart (Scrum or Kanban sheets).

Additionally, the authors of the Agile Manifesto believe that it is important to improve the description of requirements (client stories), off-base schedules (story focuses and burn to the ground), industrious asset over-burdens (supportability), and multitasking (WIP limitations).

Agile is not the only method; for example, Lean Startup, Critical Chain, and Product Development Flow are equally invested approaches. Even yet, we are aware that not all Lean processes are savvy when applied to all situations. For example, unquestionably, fabrication frameworks are distinct from item advancement frameworks, and certain Lean assembly methods don't have any impact on item advancement.

To achieve what the goal of Lean product advancements is?

Lean item advancement aims to increase the overall framework's economic throughput by means other than just pouring more money and resources into it.

Usage

If you're thinking about using it, there are two things to keep in mind:

This leads to more productive and effective advancement processes as the lean development of the item proceeds. This approach is often used nowadays while putting together organizations.

From planning through appropriation, delivery, and deals, lean progress is used across the value chain. Therefore, product designers should consider the whole framework while using Lean to avoid affecting their waste further down the line. This viewpoint is often overlooked, yet it's just as important as the first one in this debate.

There are a few fundamental methods in which Lean is used in item improvement:

❖ Visual work organizing and management improve perceptibility, co-ordination, and the flow of work.

❖ Designing a framework that incorporates the processes of learning generation, capture, and reuse

❖ Deconstructing cross-capacity and process storehouses to look at the whole value stream

❖ Encouraging groups to operate autonomously and independently by setting their schedules and priorities.

Why Lean Product Development Is Effective

Culture and practices are integrated with strategy and tools.

Many organizations are working to find ways to make improvements in execution more attainable. To improve, Lean uses a combination of group and pioneer practices, which provide organizations the tools they need to support and continuously improve execution.

Set-based designing, rapid learning cycles, boss experts, and visual organizing, such as Kanban, are common Lean Product Development methods and toolsets. Regular procedures include day-to-day executive work using visual loading up, kamishibai (monitoring the use of measures), and kaizen (continuous improvement) (improvement by everybody, all over the place, inevitably). It modifies competence and sufficiency.

Reduced inefficiency saves time and effort on tasks that don't provide value to our customers. Productive progress requires a clear understanding of which process stages provide value and which do not and the ability to eliminate or restrict those tasks that do not contribute value.

Adequacy ensures that we don't create a useless thing, even if the process is fruitful in the short term. A genuine client understanding is required to create a substantial product recommendation and a clear understanding of how to earn money from that advice for exciting advancement.

It emphasizes the importance of information gathering and dissemination.

Lean Product Development necessitates a shift in perspective to emphasize the underlying phases of the item advancement process, which are often information work stages. It necessitates a training program called "Adapting First" to help identify fundamental knowledge gaps. As groups determine which innovations will be used, information about customer connections and major risks in the proposal and business case, these learning gaps are filled by groups. This approach of information work represents a significant shift for some organizations, which are used to defining requirements as quickly as possible, selecting a concept, testing it, and stressing it from there.

Why Visual Arranging Apparatuses Are the First Step in Lean Product Development

Even a cursory examination of the methods used by Lean organizations (or by those that want to be Lean) reveals one thing in common: visual arrangement approaches.

Arranging large-scale development projects is time-consuming and difficult. Organization and task leaders devote a significant amount of effort to planning, reassessing, and implementing. Even for individuals not legally involved, such as supervisors who need to audit venture reasoning and administrators with a greater perspective of company activities, maintaining a high-level diagram of important tasks frequently proves difficult.

To create small but continuous improvements in the way groups operate, using visual methods like Kanban is an obvious and readily accessible practice.

Reduces the requirement for verbal interpretation and clarification by passing on understanding reliant on clearly visible cues such card positioning, shading, symbols, and beyond.

Even if you're just starting with visual arranging instruments, your first success may serve as a springboard for bigger and better things to come. The use of visual organizing devices enhances the clarity of findings and aids organizations in developing a strategy for managed risk-taking as part of their ongoing search for excellence.

Item improvement programming in the context of lean manufacturing?

To focus on the important things - dealing with your Hardware advancement venture - The lean item advancement venture leaders program consolidates Lean standards. It enables authorized planning as well as a day-to-day endeavor status view in Playbook. It also, as a result, re-energizes colleague-specific requirement projects when venture parameters alter throughout the organization. As a result, everyone may be sure they are doing the proper job at an appropriate moment to keep the endeavor moving forward along these lines.

Where can I get the greatest return on my Lean investment?

Knowing this, which approaches of thinking or future process improvements have the highest return on investment in typical equipment improvement frameworks? What are the alternatives? According to our findings, Visual Work Management and Project Risk Management are the two major process improvements with the highest return on investment (ROI) in most companies.

Visual Work Management and Project Risk Management offer very large ROIs when considering the Cost of Delay - effectively more than one hundred, and often more than one thousand times the cost (lost benefit due to being late to showcase). Many of these problems can be addressed considerably more quickly with minimal expense and effort if you have the finest VWM tools available for your improvement framework. You may see a demonstration of Playbook's visual work done by executives to give you a better understanding of the benefits of the visual administration tool.

What's the deal with lean item advancement?

To fully grasp lean item advancement, it helps to understand why it is used. For example, Toyota Motor Company led the way in the mid-twentieth century with lean development. To compete with the scale of American vehicle manufacturers, Toyota was remunerated with more effective frameworks that were subsequently referred to be "lean" as an additional player in the automotive industry.

Toyota's structure became more effective in the long run because it became more agile and less wasteful. Toyota's R&D, assembly, and promotion teams worked together to test, emphasize, and enhance the company's vehicles over time, in contrast to the R&D offices of American companies, which would construct a car and then throw blueprints over the infamous fence design to manufacture. In the American method, mistakes that surfaced during development sometimes make it into production and need expensive re-examination. The Toyota way that mistakes were quickly identified and corrected and the item was continually improved.

Lean assembly processes partially inspired a coordinated programming proclamation was partially inspired in the 1990s by lean assembly processes, emphasizing responding to change above a set layout.

Organizations may use the lean method to reduce waste and increase efficiency while manufacturing cars, PCs, or mobile phone apps.

Item progress according to the five lean principles

Provide the customer with a perk

Because understanding what their customers need helps organizations dispose of trash, lean item engineers concentrate on creating things that clients find useful. As long as there isn't any incentive for the customer to spend time or resources on it, it's considered waste.

For example, UX designers frequently do exhaustive customer research in the product industry and rely on volunteers, center gatherings, warning sheets, and customer testing to understand customers' preferences. Unfortunately, these tests lead people to delete information that they don't need or want.

When a client's requirements are crystal clear, item groups may begin evaluating the many arrangements that could be possible. This process is known as item revelation. It's far less costly, as Toyota learned, to test a wide range of ideas right from the start of the development process than it is to find that customers dislike the product after it has already been built. So, for example, a small business that wants to provide a product that will help large businesses attract and retain employees may consider using reviews, courses, and character assessments to achieve its goal before determining what its customers value most, such as an official information application.

Recognize the value stream and cut down on unnecessary spending

As previously stated, "Worth stream" is just a name for the methods used in the item enhancement process. Think of it as a step-by-step building process. For a car manufacturer, the process might begin with a statistical survey and conclude with the sale of a car. It's the steps a company must go through to get a functioning program into customers' hands for a product.

It used to be that every office had a little bit of the sequential construction method and didn't fully understand the roles performed by the various departments. Each group in the value stream understands its role in lean improvement, just as others know theirs. Mindfulness goes against the grain of conventional wisdom, which dictates that workers learn to master just one task before moving on to the next, yet it spurs collective innovation. Lean teams that see the broad picture are more adept at identifying waste, eliminating red tape, and creating a standardized, repeatable process.

Streamline the actions that are worth taking

Unidirectional handoffs are common in conventional progression cycles. One group will transfer work to another and consider their task accomplished. For example, consider a team of item managers that gives many structures to design and then begins working on different projects. The result is misspelled communication and a loss of focus on one's responsibilities. In addition, architects who discover flaws in the designs will be unable to go back and correct the errors they made.

All partners are involved in product improvement from the beginning with lean development. Consequently, everyone in the value chain has the opportunity to play a role in product ideation and structure at a product organization. This gives the structural group a variety of viewpoints and helps them to anticipate and prepare for potential problems down the road, such as an aspect that isn't impossible to implement after all.

As a project progresses, lean teams are concerned with pipeline administration or managing workflow to the planning and designing teams. As a result, growth is curtailed, and individuals can focus on what gives them life. The SCRUM method allocates a SCRUM Master to carry out this task in groups.

That lean teams start working before they know all of the data is important. For example, when Toyota's industrial site managers waited until a vehicle was fully designed before starting tooling machines to build the vehicle, they increased the overall improvement schedule. This was an early test for Toyota. Directors might operate in parallel and be more prepared if they begin anticipating the structural group's requirements.

Motivate and involve the people in the group

As part of the lean process, work units are given broad goals and attainable targets then left to figure things out independently. These employees are more effective in staffing and funding their activities because they better understand the requirements of the clients they serve than focal chiefs.

Cross-utilitarian thinking is common in lean organizations. For instance, a programming group for money-related administrations might include originators, architects, and item marketers so that the group can operate as an independent unit. A run is a two- or three-week period during which a shippable item is produced.

Educate yourself and become better at what you do

The process of lean item improvement requires continual learning. By catching and disseminating hierarchy learning, lean organizations avoid wasteful repetition of effort.

A wide range of hypotheses and frameworks have been proposed to help make information more widely available. For example, it supports creating learning bases or internal wikis where anybody may capture and share exercises they've learned, such as information-focused assistance (KCS).

When a company has computerized things, it may send client investigations to follow-up events to see what the customers do with their items. Those working on a wellness app, for example, might observe the Screen Flow or the typical path customers take around the app and identify areas where customers are continually encountering problems and exiting the app. Then, for a more professional and appealing customer experience, groups may organize this learning into exercises concerning where to put catches or material for a more professional and attractive encounter for clients over time.

Lean item improvement has many benefits.

When people think about lean product development, they often think of:

Reduce the length of time between improvement cycles.

Lean teams begin work before they have all of the information they need. They operate parallel with other teams to speed up the assembly process. Instead of a handoff race where one group may start work at various completions, each team covers, and races together with the lean strategy.

Lowering the cost of progress

Lean teams may identify wasteful processes and create valuable products by sharing knowledge and understanding the whole value chain. Reducing stock, getting rid of extra highlights, and creating a standardized item that can be easily changed are all part of this strategy.

Come up with innovative setups.

Workers with full data brainstorm ideas on ways to make their display better, as well as the exhibitions of their peers. For example, a lean programming building group may warn the planning group of new obstacles such as Android message pop-ups and propose alternative solutions.

Reduced production costs

Items are less costly to provide when the lean strategy is working well. It's common knowledge that reducing labor hours, devices, and support expenses is a key component of every innovative project's budget. This may also imply fewer physical materials for manufacturers.

1. Lessen redevelopment cycles by cutting costs

Getting rid of errors before they happen is a lean group's specialty as it progresses. They may make adjustments to the product while it's being produced and restructure it often to reduce problems and the frequency with which it must be redeveloped.

The Japanese assembly industry set the benchmark for lean item improvement, which is best represented by Toyota's framework, which has become recognized as the pioneer of lean techniques. To execute lean, you must go through the following five steps:

Decide how much something is worth. This is mostly determined by how much the customer is willing to spend on the product or service.

2. Identify all significant steps toward achieving respect and eliminate those that don't directly contribute to this goal.

In a short labor procedure, direct the means.

Allow the customer to evaluate and criticize the product.

Continue the cycle until the item is produced to perfection and waste is avoided at all costs.

To use lean terminology, we refer to "squander" as any activity that consumes time or money without being necessary, thereby rejecting the ethic of "work more efficiently." A few examples are: providing more of an item than the request asks for; excessive holding times between generation stages; the transportation of items not needed for production; and time wasted looking for item abandons when they might be wiped away right at the source.

Unpredictable cost-cutting should not be confused with lean item improvement. If you can't break down your current process, paying careful attention to how each step affects the final result, you'll defeat the purpose and almost certainly end up losing money. The best person to help you through the process is a certified lean specialist. Start small, with a single item or problem area, and gradually expand your lean use training to include all areas of your company. You'll soon be able to work more efficiently and earn more money than you ever imagined possible. It's important not to mistake lean product development with haphazard cost-cutting.

How to Develop a Lean Product in Five Easy Steps

Lean mindset may help reduce waste and shorten delivery times in the fast-paced world of product innovation. Using this book, you'll be able to apply lean standards to your new item advancement (NPD), make improvements to reality, and continue making supportable advancement practices for a very long time.

Although lean methods are most often used in manufacturing, they may be used in any sector since all companies benefit from process duration improvements, increased efficiency, and cost investment funds. However, there are five fundamental values in lean improvement to begin with.

- ❖ Decide on a reward for your customers
- ❖ Find out how much you're worth and focus on that
- ❖ Make a stream by removing trash.
- ❖ React to a customer request for more information
- ❖ Strive towards perfection via repetition

Show Your Customers What They Are Worth

It's critical to remember that to have a successful and cost-effective business; one must start with respect.

Before you start working on an item, look at the existing market conditions and work backward to ensure you have the product your customers will ultimately buy. With this "Market Back" strategy, you can focus your efforts on creating successful products before the generation process has even begun.

The word "client" isn't always inclusive. Clients may be divided into internal clients (those who work for your organization) and external clients (the individuals who will purchase your item).

A sure-fire way to find out what your customers find important and will finally buy is to try a lot and evaluate quickly. This involves getting rid of failures quickly, not wasting time trying to turn a washout into a winner, and staying one step ahead of your competition by being very agile in all of your efforts.

Persuading colleagues to choose transportation above productivity may be your toughest challenge. It doesn't matter how good your development is if you don't have the right product available for customers at the right moment.

You must keep your teams focused on the processes, which are often referred to as the worth stream while determining value.

Realize Your Value Stream and Concentrate on It

The development of an item has ramifications for the whole biological system of your association. To ensure that a product can be shown successfully, it is essential to plan from start to end and ensure that all the participants in the company know their roles. To name just a few, associations operate more smoothly when everyone in the value stream understands their role in the process.

Conventional promotion processes consisted of numerous 'hand-offs' across divisions, resulting in various communication errors and no clear way to differentiate between upgrades. As soon as a product was developed in R&D, it was handed over to assembly, who was responsible for putting it into action.

Lean item improvement flips this approach on its head. Partnering with a lean approach means that everyone is on the same page and aligned from the start, so there are no handoffs or curveballs to deal with.

When people work together at the beginning of a project, the number of accidents and robberies as the project moves along is reduced. In addition, extending the timeline considers problems that need to be identified and resolved ahead of time not to affect the project's deliverability later.

Showing concurrent improvement plans may assist in visualizing this. You'll see that R&D isn't immediately pushed to the side with this structure. Instead, issues in the commercial center may be identified and quickly resolved by staying needed throughout the dispatch while maintaining a laser focus on providing some value for your customers.

The emphasis on value allows your teams to remove advancements that don't add value, but it also reduces waste, which leads directly to the next step of your lean process – stream.

Reduce Waste to Improve Flow

Why does a lean company need ever-increasing flow rates for processes and value streams? If processes flow, customers will be serviced faster, lead times will be shorter, item quality will increase, and you'll become more flexible, as the list goes on.

A faster stream, for instance, equates to reduced item costs.

A lean organization recognizes that the price of a product is largely influenced by how quickly it moves through the value stream. To speed up the process, what has to be done? Identify what involves and does not include respect and what tasks may be accomplished concurrently without regard for circumstances by thinking through the process.

Respond to a customer's request

Understanding customer appeal is critical to accelerating the rate at which items progress. Therefore, when a customer requests a product, destroy the focal point through which the streams are viewed and evaluated for ongoing improvements.

You enhance the customer experience by removing waste and streamlining processes, and you free up time to focus on tasks with a higher value. It's important to remember that drawing doesn't mean rushing through processes. In its place, however, it gives you the ability to respond quickly to customer requirements by fostering a more actively engaged workforce.

As a result, your organization must stay on top of processes and generate data to respond quickly when a pull is applied. As a result, these businesses may make a significant contribution to the management of earnings.

When less money and space is invested in crude goods, your organization will be better positioned to respond quickly to the demands of your customers and make greater use of your enhanced revenue streams. Time spent approving a client's interest may also be used to clear up estimation and uncertainty for future projects.

Repeat your efforts until you achieve perfection.

Redundancy is the cornerstone of lean product development. The process of defining worth, setting up esteem streams, removing waste, and presenting both the stream and the draw may be repeated until a state of flawlessness is reached, generating measurable reward with no waste.

When you follow lean item advancement criteria, you can have it all: fast delivery, high productivity, and high quality. However, if you're not focused on the main issue, it will be far more difficult to make a business case for your lean activity throughout the item improvement cycle. In addition, it would help if you kept a close eye on your results once you've implemented lean item advancement to maintain board support for it.

Fortunately, when you improve your processes, the results will improve as well, and your customers will see the benefits.

Lean Product and Process Development's primary goal is to provide the high-quality product that people want. In addition, faster market entry of clearly superior products implies future productivity. This is achieved by generating reusable learning that can be used in the future, emphasizing an item and transmitting set-based simultaneous construction, which is what lean product advancement does (which involves considering sets of structures on the double to rapidly wipe out second rate arrangements, therefore shortening improvement times). The coordination of engineers' work with that of the assembly office is also beneficial. As a result, the shop floor receives a well-researched, botch-proof item ready for production without extensive and expensive modification.

A lean approach to planning improvements

The ideal PD process should function similarly to an assembly line's single-piece stream, speaking to a value stream from inception to production, without interruptions due to inefficiency or a need to go back and correct errors. If you're using PD, obtaining the right data at the right time may be more important than completing the right exercises (or avoiding doing the wrong ones).

The planning approach depicted here uses lean standards to infer a project movement structure that relies on a value creation sequenced set of affirmation events that only pulls the basic and adequate data and materials from the item improvement group because of significant worth creation and waste reduction. There are four steps to the intended method:

(Value assurance: this method describes the Value Breakdown Structure (VBS) since it uses the item vision as information. Compared to a normal WBS, the VBS breaks down the job into smaller and increasingly comprehensible parts. At the same time, the latter provides an incentive to the partners in unambiguous criteria, which are referred to as valuable items. Therefore, use this process instead of the PMBOK's "Extension Definition" and "Make WBS" steps.

It prioritizes the most fundamental item modules or hierarchical processes that a large number of choices will produce. (2) Set-based Concurrent Engineering (SBCE) Hazard Identification, Hazard Qualitative Analysis, Hazard Quantitative Analysis, and Hazard Response Planning are included in this process from the PMBOK guide.

An item, component, service, or data should never be sent along the value stream without a direct request from the following forms. Physical advancement confirmations (i.e., models, models, generational starting, and so on) are linked to the dismantling events, which are important minutes for information capture. Distinct from tall doors where data bunches are created, pull occasions guarantee the value stream, make quality problems apparent, and produce information in the process. Using the PMBOK's "Action Definition" and "Action Sequencing" forms, stages 3 and 4 put the project into action.

This series of value creation activities are described and executed following the force occasions.

CHAPTER EIGHT

ARTIFICIAL INTELLIGENCE AND PROCUREMENT

Despite its popularity, artificial intelligence (AI) is a relatively new potential for Procurement departments.

Artificial intelligence (AI) is often portrayed as a panacea for all of humanity's ills. Unfortunately, too much emphasis is placed on future possibilities rather than current business realities.

If you want to avoid the hype around artificial intelligence, this approach may help. Many explanations and examples are provided for Procurement professionals unfamiliar with the subject matter before reading this guide.

What is procurement's use of artificial intelligence (AI)?

Procurement companies may use artificial intelligence to tackle difficult issues more quickly and effectively. In addition, numerous software applications, from expenditure monitoring to contract administration and strategic sourcing, may be enhanced using artificial intelligence (AI).

Since the 1950s, academics have studied artificial intelligence, but it has only lately found practical uses in procurement. The broadest definition of artificial intelligence (AI) is a collection of emerging computer technologies that can learn and adjust their behavior. In most cases, artificial intelligence (AI) software is designed to do a job better or more quickly than a person can.

AI that is both strong and narrow.

Strong AI, sometimes known as artificial general intelligence in popular culture, is frequently depicted (AGI.) For example, two classic science fiction films, Terminator and I, Robot, portray robots as intelligent enough to perform human-like duties.

However, all currently known uses of artificial intelligence in procurement represent a limited form of the technology known as weak AI. They're interested in innovative solutions to extremely narrowly defined problems. Despite these limitations, narrow AI has the potential to improve operational efficiency in the short term.

In procurement, what does artificial intelligence not entail?

Artificial intelligence is shrouded in myth and misinformation. According to Procurement experts, artificial intelligence (AI) isn't the chrome- or plastic-plated sentient creature you see in movies. Instead of replacing human procurement knowledge, it should be viewed as a new team member capable of promoting organizational transformation, strategic sourcing, or actual savings. Procurement should not look at artificial intelligence (AI) as a miraculous answer to their issues. All current Procurement AI solutions require active professional supervision and direction.

What does procurement's use of artificial intelligence entail?

Procurement, meanwhile, is already being transformed by artificial intelligence. Using artificial intelligence, procurement professionals may save time by automating or enhancing time-consuming processes while gaining insights from massive amounts of complex data. To put it another way, artificial intelligence (AI) may be thought of as a software solution designed to do a particular job. However, because artificial intelligence (AI) is just software, it can quickly alter working habits in even huge companies. Therefore, consider AI as a new kind of software rather than simply another buzzword.

Definitions of Artificial Intelligence in the Procurement Process

Artificial intelligence (AI) refers to any software solution that incorporates self-learning, intelligent algorithms when it comes to procurement. Throughout the tutorial, examples and definitions will be provided.

Algorithms that show behavior that is deemed "smart" are believed to be using artificial intelligence (AI). In the field of artificial intelligence, this is known as machine learning (ML).

Computer algorithms that understand, alter, and create human language are called Natural Language Processing (NLP).

Automation of repetitive, basic activities using robots (RPA): algorithms that imitate human behaviors. RPA isn't usually thought of as an application of artificial intelligence (AI).

Algorithms are used in all types of artificial intelligence because they describe how to solve a particular issue. Most computer software is built on algorithms, which anybody with a strong mathematical background can compute. It is impossible to see the work done by algorithms in software, but professionals can program and re-program them to address significant issues in software settings.

While RPA gives Procurement numerous possibilities to enhance process efficiency, it should not be called artificial intelligence. Instead, it's easier to understand if you think of RPA as artificial intelligence (AI) software robot mimics human behavior.

Some Procurement Use Cases for Artificial Intelligence

While AI usage in commercial applications is still in its infancy, procurement operations are increasingly using AI. The following are some of the most popular strategies:

Classification of Spending

Spend may be divided into several categories and sub-categories using machine learning techniques. Reviewing millions of invoices, for example, to automatically classify spending in various cardboard packaging categories.

Comparing and contrasting different suppliers

Invoice and purchase order data may be linked to a vendor hierarchy using machine learning to make the connection. Connecting a freight and logistics company's many local subsidiaries to a single worldwide supplier, as one example.

Getting Data from a Supplier or the Market

Find and collect data about suppliers or particular marketplaces using methods such as natural language processing. Monitoring social media platforms, for example, for indications regarding the risk situations of suppliers.

Detection of Unusual Behavior

Automatic detection and surfacing of information related to procurement using machine learning techniques Unexpected fluctuations in commodity or supplier purchasing prices, for example.

Purchasing Artificial Intelligence (AI) Software

In 2018, 45 percent of Chief Procurement Officers utilized or piloted artificial intelligence software, according to Deloitte. Here are seven typical areas in the procurement cycle where artificial intelligence (AI) may be utilized.

Management of Supplier Risks

Artificial intelligence may be used to keep an eye on the supply chain and spot any possible problems. Many big data methods are utilized in risk management software, such as RiskMethods RiskIntelligence, to filter and give warnings for millions of various data sources.

Using AI to Make Software Purchases

Purchase orders may be automatically reviewed and approved using artificial intelligence. The Tradeshift platform, for example, features a chatbot named Ada that can automatically authorize virtual card payments or monitor the progress of transactions.

Automation of the accounts payable process

Accounts payable automation is increasingly using machine learning. Automated payment processes that utilize machine learning, such as samples, speed up payment processing while detecting fraud.

Software for AI-based Expenditure Analysis

Automatic expenditure categorization and vendor matching are two examples of machine learning algorithms in procurement spend analysis.

Identification of a brand-new Provider

Big data techniques provide new avenues for locating, analyzing, and using supplier information from both public and private sources. Platforms like Tealbook use machine learning to improve supplier discovery based on data that has been gleaned, cleaned, and enhanced from the web.

Strategic Sourcing with the Aid of Artificial Intelligence

Managing and automating sourcing events may also be accomplished with the help of artificial intelligence (AI). For example, it utilizes machine learning to recognize bid sheets and includes eSourcing bots for different categories, including raw materials and maintenance/repair.

Software for Contract Management

When it comes to contract management, artificial intelligence offers a lot of potential applications. Natural language processing, for example, allows software like Seal Software to read and analyze long and verbose legal documents automatically in search of cost savings possibilities.

Using Procurement Data to Train an AI

Most commercial applications of artificial intelligence require human oversight. For example, supervised learning is most often used in AI procurement applications. Procurement specialists are often brought in to help robots learn how to do a certain job.

Here's how procurement data may be used to train artificial intelligence:

Training data collection is provided to an artificial intelligence system with a particular task as the initial step 1. For example, to give you an idea, you might look at how 100,000 bills were divided into various spending categories.

As soon as you have a goal in mind, you can start supplying the AI system with unclassified Procurement data to categorize according to the logic it has seen in the training data.

When AI is confident in its ability to identify data properly, it will do so without requiring any input from the user.

Procurement specialists would evaluate categorization choices in situations where AI did not have a high level of confidence. This procedure is referred to as "human annotation" in certain circles.

Procurement Data would be categorized and used to actively train the AI system to identify future data with the help of human assessments.

More data would be classified automatically over time, but the quality of data categorization based on human input would also increase.

As a Procurement organization, think about the tasks at hand with adequate training data, a requirement to handle unclassified data reliably, and a clear output that provides value to the company.

Examine a few situations in which artificial intelligence (AI) may be beneficial to the procurement process.

Use of Artificial Intelligence (AI) in Sourcing

Artificial intelligence (AI) excels at tackling complicated issues requiring huge data and precisely defined success metrics. Harvard Corporate Review and Deloitte recently researched the main areas where business leaders anticipate

AI's most success. They found that each company has its unique set of problems and possibilities, and these are the areas where artificial intelligence (AI) may provide value to procurement.

The following are some key areas where artificial intelligence (AI) may assist in procurement:

- ❖ Artificial intelligence (AI) can offer fast analytics and data-driven insights to help companies source more effectively.

- ❖ Make smarter choices.

- ❖ Artificial intelligence (AI) may find new ways to save money or make money by sifting through large quantities of data.

- ❖ AI can simplify or harmonize internal business processes in big companies with different business divisions or geographical locations.

- ❖ Using AI to automate manual activities, such as monthly procedures or procurement performance reports, may save a great deal of time.

- ❖ Allow procurement personnel to focus on more creative or strategic activities, such as managing important supplier relationships.

- ❖ Free up time.

Artificial intelligence (AI) may assist procurement companies in capturing important new sources of data, such as those found on the Internet or other external data sources.

With access to large quantities of external data, artificial intelligence (AI) may assist in identifying new suppliers or new markets to join.

Provider relationship management may be made more data-informed with the use of artificial intelligence (AI).

Procurement and Machine Learning

Artificial intelligence (AI) includes machine learning (ML), which has direct use in procurement. Automated or autonomous procurement procedures have a logical descendant in robotic process automation (RPA).

A key misunderstanding about artificial intelligence (AI) in procurement is the role of machine learning. Unfortunately, there's much misunderstanding about what "machine learning in procurement" really means. The term "machine learning" may refer to various techniques, from simple regression to complex logistic regression. It's time to debunk a few misconceptions about machine learning by going through the fundamentals.

Automated statistics that learn from their behavior are used in procurement to address specific problems or enhance operational efficiency. Automated statistics can be compared to RPA. However, RPA is not capable of learning and improving over time.

Machines That Can Learn Different Things (From A Procurement Context)

As ML becomes more widely utilized in procurement, it needs increasing levels of human involvement.

With Supervised Learning, a pattern-detection algorithm learns from previous data and applies it to new data. Algorithms are taught to look for patterns in data by having people give accurate responses. Frequently used in procurement, for example, in the categorization of expenditures.

Data Mining: the algorithm searches for new and intriguing patterns in previously unknown data. Unsupervised Learning: In the absence of supervision, the algorithm is not intended to surface particular right answers but rather to search for logical patterns in the raw data. In essential procurement functions, this term is rarely used.

Learning through Reinforcement: the algorithm determines how to behave in specific circumstances, and the behavior is rewarded or penalized based on the outcomes. In the context of procurement, this is mostly theoretical.

Brain-inspired Deep Learning uses artificial neural networks to improve their performance on a task over time. As a result, procurement departments have a new chance to seize.

Spend Classification and Analysis Using Machine Learning

Data-intensive operations like procurement analytics already utilize machine learning extensively. Consider how machine learning is utilized in spend analytics, particularly how it may be used to solve the categorization problem is spend analytics.

What's Wrong with Spending?

Procurement expenditure classification is a long-standing issue, and it's also one of the first uses of artificial intelligence that's seen wide adoption today.

Many procurement organizations are challenged by the requirement to classify millions of unique transactions based on data from invoices, purchase orders, or other data sources into procurement categories of procurement. The best-intentioned Procurement companies build elaborate hierarchies of categories and subcategories, but they run into problems when classifying new data or keeping the quality or speed up. For example, most procurement companies used to look at their spending once or twice a year. Still, today's high-performing Procurement businesses use near real-time data updates to keep up with business demands.

Another issue is that the quantity of data accessible from various sources rises, and connecting heterogeneous data sources becomes more difficult. For example, procurement organizations use many ERP systems, purchase-to-pay solutions, and other finance-related technologies to collect expenditure data. There may only be a few relevant data points in each source system. Thus different expenditure data must be linked together into a single hierarchy.

In the general ledger, a new Dell computer, for example, could be listed as IT equipment, but in the invoice line description, it's described as a laptop computer. An alternative description relating to a vendor or maker-specific data points may also be included in the purchase order for this item. Even though all of these sources point to the same thing, correctly classifying it takes insight.

Classification of Procurement Spend Using AI

Various elements of artificial intelligence (AI) have promise when it comes to spending categorization, but most software solutions today still rely on supervised machine learning. Using Sievo's spend analytics, let's have a look at a real example of machine learning-powered expenditure categorization in action:

- ❖ Machine learning algorithms can categorize new expenditure data into procurement taxonomies automatically as a starting point.

- ❖ A categorization function in the program may also provide recommendations to category specialists.

- In addition, the AI-classifier driven by machine learning may provide a confidence level ranging from 0 to 1. A low level of confidence is around zero, while a higher number represents a greater confidence level.

- Machine learning is also capable of classifying new expenditures. Rule-based classifications produced by human category specialists may be detected using this technology.

For future classifications, a human category expert may offer important training input by reviewing or validating material that has been AI-classified.

Artificial Intelligence for Procurement in Natural Language

Artificial intelligence, a field known as natural language processing (NLP), studies how computers can better comprehend, interpret, and even manipulate human language. As a result, NLP may unearth fresh insights from current data or open up previously inefficient procedures when it comes to procurement. Let's look at some real-world instances to see what I mean.

Incorporating NLP into the Management of Contracts

There is a wealth of information in legal contracts for procurement, such as termination dates, payment conditions, and rights to renegotiation. Unfortunately, procurement teams haven't had easy access to this data in the past since contracts were drafted in contractual language and kept offline or on shared internet files without the data included in them. However, through a technique known as text parsing, natural language processing has allowed procurement to mine contracts for useful data. Contract management software can read and understand huge volumes of contracts quickly and effectively using parsing algorithms. Optical character recognition (OCR) technology is an even more advanced method, which uses artificial intelligence to recognize text in pictures, even images of previously undigitized scanned contracts.

Embedding Words in Invoice Headers and Footers

Machine learning algorithms and artificial intelligence (AI) programs are considerably better at understanding numerical data than humans are. For example, computers think in binary systems (ones and zeroes), while people think about words. Using NLP's word embedding technique, words and phrases in a vocabulary are mapped according to how closely they resemble or relate to one another. For example, with the analysis of purchase order text fields, word embedding may help procurement discover groupings of bought goods that fall into the same category or subcategory, thus saving time and money.

Chatbot Natural Language Generation

Artificial intelligence (AI) applications that use natural language generation, such as chatbots and personal assistants, are hot topics right now (NLG). NLP is furthered by these systems, which first analyze user input before providing a textual story in response. Siri, Alexa, and Google Assistant are already extensively utilized in consumer applications. Still, NLG is presently restricted to pre-configured chatbots or virtual assistants that perform just a small number of activities.

Purchasing with a Mindset

New terminology and meanings are being created as a result of the introduction of brand-new technology. "Cognitive procurement" has been a popular new term in the procurement industry in recent years.

Exactly what is Cognitive Procurement, and why is it important?

Artificial intelligence methods like automated data mining, machine learning, pattern recognition, and NLP are utilized in the procurement environment to imitate human intelligence in cognitive procurement. The name comes from "cognitive computing," a new area of sophisticated computer science.

Cognizant Information Technology

When we talk about cognitive computing, we're talking about anything that works like the human brain and helps us make better decisions. It mimics how the human brain perceives, thinks, and responds to stimuli to tackle particular tasks or difficulties.

Analytical Thinking

Cognitive analytics, a kind of cognitive computing, may have applications in procurement (CA). By simulating the human brain's capacity to perceive patterns and draw inferences from data. While cognitive analytics may address many procurement analytics problems, this is not always the case when using AI-assisted analytics.

Outsourcing with a Cognitive Approach

Assisting in sourcing procedures is another way cognitive computers may help Procurement. When used correctly, cognitive sourcing may assist buyers and procurement teams to identify new possibilities and automate non-strategic sourcing tasks. Cognitive sourcing may be shown through sourcing aids like chatbots.

Cognitive Procurement Challenges

Because cognitive computing is a young area, care is advised while pursuing it. As of 2019, there is still disagreement about what defines "cognitive" processes in the business context and what fundamental definitions are. Meanwhile, many software solutions on the market claim to have an intellect similar to a human person. Therefore, despite rapid advancements in technology, it is suggested that assumptions made in cognitive procurement be verified by information systems specialists, whether internal or external.

Procurement Best Practices Using Artificial Intelligence

Even the most difficult tasks begin with a single tiny step. Procurement leaders may begin using artificial intelligence by following some tried-and-true best practices that we've compiled. Our Procurement AI Game Plan, which is 11 pages long, contains more best practices.

Begin by tackling the most mundane issues first.

First, while using AI, don't expect any magical changes in how your Procurement activities are conducted. Don't treat artificial intelligence (AI) as some kind of enchanted new elixir. Instead, consider AI from the perspective of the business process. Even the most routine company activities can be time-consuming and resource-intensive to handle if you think about it. Embedding AI technology into current processes – such as spending analysis or contract management – will provide instant benefit over building new applications out of it in the future.

Gather as much information as possible.

It's also a good idea to gather as much Procurement-related data as possible before you know what to do with it. Don't wait for the data to be perfect before using it. Instead, use artificial intelligence (AI) to assist you in understanding and enhancing the quality of historical data over time. The goal is to increase the amount of data that artificial intelligence can process. Providing AI with a larger amount of data will result in higher training outcomes.

Provide AI with specific problems to solve.

Artificial intelligence (AI) and machine learning (ML) are now excellent for a small number of limited use-cases. For example, invoice line items can be used for machine learning to classify Procurement costs. However, AI is unlikely to handle complicated supplier negotiations. Look for activities that don't take much of your procurement team's time but have a big impact on the team's overall success while doing them.

Be willing to try new things.

Artificial intelligence (AI) has great promise for improving procurement performance in the long term. Be willing to try new things. Consider presenting problems and training samples from your data to experts in developing artificial intelligence (AI) technologies. Don't be afraid to make errors. Learn from them, and keep your eye on the prize. Finally, recognize that technology advances rapidly. Thus today's unsuccessful trials may be feasible with tomorrow's new artificial intelligence techniques.

Make it possible for humans and machines to work together

Finally, keep in mind that any use of AI in Procurement would need procurement specialists who can provide active direction and assistance. Think about how your procurement team's skills may be enhanced rather than replaced by artificial intelligence by working with machines. To get the most out of both human and machine intelligence, be a change agent.

Bonus

Smart Contracts in Blockchain

INTRODUCING SMART CONTRACTS

One of the most notable features of blockchain is decentralization — that is, it is capable of being shared among all entities of the blockchain network, so removing the participation of third-party intermediaries or intermediaries or third parties. This feature is beneficial because it keeps you from the likelihood of any process conflict while time-saving. Thus, while the blockchain technology is not perfect in their entirety, they provide quicker, inexpensive and more compelling opportunities in comparison to traditional banking systems. Owing to this fact, even governmental organizations and corporate financial institutions are now shifting to the blockchain.

Recently, the most used application of blockchain technology is something called "smart contracts." Conceptualized by cryptographer and legal scholar Nick Szabo, the idea of a smart contract was born in 1994. Szabo concluded that any decentralized ledger could be used as smart contracts, which means these contracts will be self-executable and digital. By converting these digital contracts into code, they could then be executed on a blockchain.

While the concept of smart contracts had been around more than two decades ago, our present-day system functions on paper-based contracts. When digital contracts even come into play, they will still involve a trusted third party, which is essential. And although we have managed to work out the rules and regulations of paper-based contracts, their effectiveness and smoothness cannot be relied on. If a third party is involved in any contract, the transactional fee has increased the risk of fraudulent activities or securities problems increases as well.

So as blockchain takes foot in the digital technology landscape, these issues can now be effectively addressed. A blockchain-based system permits all the parties in the network to relate with each other in a distributed way, therefore removing the obligation of trusted third parties.

Simply put: blockchain is a technology capable of storing data on a distributed ledger. This stored data of transactions and records are available in real-time to all the entities in the network. Like Bitcoin, the leading and most recognized form of cryptocurrency to date, became a buzzword in digital work, blockchain technology started garnering the attention of mainstream media. Apart from its application in cryptocurrency, blockchain has advanced, spreading its seamless benefits across several industries.

Smart contracts are practical applications of blockchain technology, and when used instead of traditional contracts, they can lower the transaction costs considerably. The most well-known blockchain platform for the creation of smart contracts is called "Ethereum."

Developed in 2016, Ethereum is built on a feature known as "Turing-completeness," which permits creating more custom-made smart contracts. As a result, smart contracts apply across several fields and industries, from asset management to real estate to e-commerce to even smart homes.

By definition, a smart contract is a computer code between two or more entities run on blockchain technology, consisting of a set of fixed rules agreed upon by the participating entities. As the smart contract is executed, it will generate the needed output if these fixed rules are met.

A smart contract is built on a computer code that permits decentralized automation, which facilitates, verifies, and enforces the conditions of the principal agreement made by two or more parties. So if you want to exchange valuables, like property, shares, or even money, smart contracts will assist you in doing so transparently while removing the presence of a middleman (or third party), thus making the process free of conflict.

If we are to follow the traditional process of obtaining a court-registered document as proof, we would have first to seek the services of a notary or an attorney, paying them for their services and waiting until the paper is delivered. But with the rise of contracts, the status quo has changed totally. Thus, if we were to go the route of smart contracts, we would obtain the necessary documents by simply paying for them without involving third parties, like notaries or attorneys. Furthermore, smart contracts are not restricted to merely outlining the rules around an agreement but are also in charge of automatically implementing those obligations and regulations.

The vending machine analogy

A simple way of explaining smart contracts is by comparing the technology to a vending machine. Customarily, we would go to an attorney or a notary, pay them, and wait to obtain the document. With smart contracts, we would slip a Bitcoin into the vending machine (which stands as a ledger), and whatever needed document enters our account. In addition, smart contracts outline the penalties and rules concerning an agreement (just like the traditional contract does) and implement those responsibilities automatically.

Self-executable, self-verifiable and tamper-proof, smart contracts typically work on a system that comprises digital assets with several parties; in this case, the involved entities can all oversee their investments. They can choose to either deposit these assets or redistribute among the other parties as stated to the obligation of the contract. Because of the lack of a third-party and the ability to track the performance of assets on smart contracts in real-time, they are relatively cheaper and safer.

Real estate analogy

Another simple analogy for explaining smart contracts is the real estate business. For instance, say you have a property to sell — and the process of doing so requires several paperwork and hours of talks between several parties. Apart from the problem of communication, every contract will likely comprise the risk of fraudulent activities. In our present times, anybody willing to sell their home or apartment will do so by seeking the services of a real estate agent. These agents serve as middlemen in the entire process by working on negotiations and supervising the deal.

Since, in a situation like this, you cannot fully trust the other party you are selling to, the real estate agent would bring in the involvement of escrow services — they will be responsible for transferring the payment from one party to another party. Once the deal has reached finalization, you would need to make payments to both the real estate agents and the escrow services — in terms of commissions and percentages initially agreed upon. Therefore, in selling your property, you are losing more money and even taking more risks.

With the introduction of smart contracts, these issues can easily be worked out effectively. Blockchain-based smart contracts are made to function solely based on agreed-upon conditions. That is, the property can quickly be passed over to the buyer once they have fulfilled the requirements (payments and terms) that you have both agreed upon. So instead of depending on escrow services, a notable cheaper alternative is a smart contract.

In smart contracts, both the payment and the right of ownership are kept in a distributed ledger system, and the details are accessible in real-time to all the parties associated with the deal. By using a smart contract system, you will remove the need for a real estate agent or any third party for that matter. Of course, compared to your traditional options, you would be saving a significant amount of time and money with a digital contract.

Remember

As established, a smart contract is automatically responsible for the executing lines of code, which are stored on a blockchain network, built around a set of rules made by the parties involved. If these rules are met, these codes are charged with executing autonomously and providing the output. Therefore, smart contracts play an essential role in business deals and collaborations, which are worked around agreed terms by two or more consenting parties. By converting contracts into computer code, this format allows the code to be kept and replicated on the system — allowing it to be managed by a computer network that runs on blockchain. In addition, whenever valuables (money or assets) are transferred and received on this network, ledger feedback is available for all parties to see, thus ensuring transparency.

UNDERSTANDING BLOCKCHAIN TECHNOLOGY

Before we can go deep into the exciting world of smart contracts, we need to understand its foundation: blockchain technology. Our society is run by technology today. And with the rising demand for innovation in our everyday lives, more and more people are taking up new technology. From voice recognition software to augmented reality to artificial intelligence (AI) virtual assistants, this new technology has made our lives more accessible over the last decade. And with the acceptance of blockchain technology, the way we do things is bound to get easier.

As established, a blockchain is a chain of blocks that contains information or data. Despite being invented earlier, the first practical and widespread application of blockchain technology began in 2009 — by Satoshi Nakamoto. Using blockchain technology, he made the first digital cryptocurrency and termed it "Bitcoin."

Blockchain, an innovative technology that impacts several industries astonishingly, was first presented to the mainstream media when Bitcoin came into prominence. Bitcoin is simply a type of cryptocurrency (digital currency) that can be used instead of officially sanctioned money for transactions. And the principal technology which leads to the attainment of cryptocurrencies is blockchain.

There is a widespread mistaken belief among people that blockchain and Bitcoin mean the same thing. But the truth is far from that. Making cryptocurrencies is just one of the many blockchain applications, and apart from Bitcoin, we have several other applications running on blockchain technology.

Simply put, blockchain is a global database consisting of transactional records; it is a data structure thus is secure, transparent, and decentralized. Blockchain can also be expressed like a chain of records (kept in blocks) supervised by no distinct authority. In other words, it is a distributed ledger that is entirely open to every party on the network. When information is kept on a blockchain, it is tough (if not impossible) to alter or manipulate it.

Every blockchain-based transaction is protected with a digital signature which shows its legitimacy. Because of digital signatures and encryption, the data kept on the blockchain cannot be tampered with or altered.

Blockchain technology permits all the parties in a network to agree, generally called a "consensus." Every data deposited on a blockchain is digitally logged and has a shared history accessible by all the parties in the network. Due to this, the likelihood of duplicitous activities and falsified transactions is removed. Moreover, there is no need for a third party in every transaction because of its decentralization feature.

For a more straightforward breakdown of how blockchain works, think about this instance: you are trying to send funds to someone who lives in another country, and you are considering your options. The traditional way is to use either your bank or an online payment transfer service such as PayPal. With all these conventional methods, a third party (local bank or PayPal) is required to help with the transaction. So, either as a transfer charge or fee, additional cash is deducted by the third party. Apart from incurring extra costs in traditional cases, you cannot guarantee the safety of your cash as it is very likely that a cyber attacker might interrupt the network and take your hard-earned cash. Either way, the customer will eventually bear the brunt. Therefore, blockchain plays a vital role.

So rather than utilizing a local bank for cash transactions, we can instead use blockchain to escape the problems and risks of the traditional ways — a more straightforward and more secure form of banking. Likewise, no additional fee is needed because the money is processed by the participants directly, removing the involvement of a third party. And since decentralization is a significant feature of the blockchain database, it is not restricted to any one location. This means that all the records and information stored on the blockchain are decentralized and public. Moreover, as the information is never deposited in one place, there is no likelihood of corrupted information even by the best hackers.

How blockchain works

Information is stored on every block in the blockchain network, with each block containing the hash of its preceding block. By definition, a hash is an exclusive mathematical code belonging to a particular block. Therefore, if the information within a block is altered, the block's hash will also have to undergo alteration. Thus, this linking of blocks via exclusive hash keys gives blockchain strong protection.

Although transactions occur on a blockchain, we have designated network "nodes" responsible for validating each transaction. These nodes use the model of "proof-of-work" in processing and validating every transaction on the network. For a transaction to be validated, each block must correlate with the hash of the previous block. In this case, the transaction will only occur if the hash is accurate. For example, suppose a cyber attacker tries to hack the network and alter information on any particular block. In that case, the hash connected to the block will also have to be subjected to modification. This breach can be easily discovered if the altered hash does not match up with the other ones. Thus, this system guarantees that the blockchain is unchangeable because any alteration performed on the series of blocks will be mirrored through the whole network and, of course, will be easily discovered.

A breakdown of a blockchain transaction

❖ A blockchain network uses private or public keys so as create a digital signature that guarantees consent and security for every transaction.

❖ After authentication is done via these keys, authorization is also required.

❖ Blockchain permits parties of the network to do mathematical authentications and come to a consensus, therefore agreeing on any specific value.

❖ In transferring something, the sender will use their private key, announcing the transaction information throughout the network. After this, a block contains information like the receiver's public key, timestamp, and digital signature.

❖ This information block is then announced throughout the network, initiating the process of validation.

❖ Network-wide miners (people who create Bitcoins) begin to solve the mathematical problem linked to the transaction to process this transaction. To solve this puzzle, miners require computers with extremely high processing power and high electrical power usage.

❖ When a miner becomes the first to solve a puzzle, they are rewarded with Bitcoins — this process is called "mining." And this type of puzzle (mathematical problems) is called the proof-of-work

❖ Immediately most network nodes reach a consensus, agreeing to a mutual answer. Then, the system timestamps the block and includes it in the current blockchain. This block can comprise any information — from messages to data to even cash.

❖ Once the new block is linked to the blockchain, the older blockchain copies are kept up to date.

Features of blockchain

The following features keep the groundbreaking technology of blockchain unique:

1. Decentralized: Blockchains are decentralized. This means that nobody or group has absolute control of the entire network. Although every network participant owns a replica of the distributed ledger, not one person can modify it alone. This exclusive feature of blockchain gives room for security and transparency while granting power to all parties — because everyone is equal.

2. Peer-to-peer network: Because of the way blockchain is set up, a peer-to-peer interaction between two parties is straightforwardly done without the need for intermediaries. Blockchain makes use of P2P protocol that permits all parties in the network to own the identical copy of transactions, allowing consent via a mechanized consensus. Take, for instance, if you want to perform a transaction in another country, you can use blockchain to do it quickly. Besides, any additional charges or interruptions will not be removed during the transfer process.

3. Immutability: The immutability feature of a blockchain means that data entered on the blockchain can never be altered or deleted. To comprehend immutability, consider the process of sending an email. When you send a broadcast email to 5,000 recipients, you cannot retract it. If you want to get rid of that email, you will need to tell every recipient to get rid of it, which is a pretty tedious process.

Therefore, immediately a data is processed on the blockchain, it can never be changed or altered. And even when you attempt to change the data one bock, you will need to modify the whole blockchain because each block keeps the hash of its previous block. Therefore, an alteration in one hash will cause a modification in all the subsequent hashes. It is tremendously difficult for anyone to alter all the hashes because it demands much computational power to perform this. Therefore, any data kept in a blockchain is immutable — free of cyberattacks or changes.

4. Cannot be tampered with: Because of the immutability feature fixed in blockchains, detecting the meddling of data is very easy. Tamper-proof and safe, any change (even in one block) in a blockchain will be easily spotted and tackled swiftly. To detect the meddling of data, the blocks and hashes are studied.

As we have established, each hash function (linked with a block) is exclusive to that block. It is more or less the "fingerprint" of that block. Therefore, any modification in the data will cause a change in the hash function. And because one block's hash function is connected to that of the following block, if a cyber attacker is going to perform any alterations, they must have to alter the hashes of all the other blocks — this is extremely difficult for anyone to do.

Kinds of blockchains

While blockchain seemed to have advanced and spread into different works of life, there are two major types of blockchains classification: private blockchain and public blockchain.

Before we head toward the dissimilarity between these two, let us see the parallels between a private blockchain and a public blockchain:

- ❖ Both private and public blockchain has decentralized P2P networks
- ❖ All the parties in the network own an identical copy of the shared ledger.
- ❖ Via a consensus, the network is responsible for maintaining the duplicates of the ledger and synchronizing the newest update.
- ❖ The rules for the safety and immutability of the ledger are agreed upon and used on the network to prevent malicious attacks.

Since we understand the similarities between these blockchains, let us explain their differences.

1. Public blockchain: This is a ledger that requires no permission, so it is accessible by anybody at any time. As long as this person can access the Internet, they are authorized to obtain and access a public blockchain. Furthermore, anyone can as well see the entire blockchain history as well as make transactions via it. Public blockchains typically compensate the parties in their network for carrying out the process of mining and preserving the ledger's immutability. Bitcoin is one prominent example of a public blockchain.

Public blockchains permit a global community of users to share information securely and freely. Nevertheless, a clear drawback is a possibility of being negatively affected if the agreed-upon rules are not implemented firmly. Besides, the rules agreed upon and applied at the outset have a minimal scope of adjustment in the future stages.

2. Private Blockchain: They are exclusively shared among trusted parties. The owners control the entire supervision of the network. Also, the rules of the private blockchain can be altered according to several factors such as authorization, members count, exposure and levels of permissions, and more.

Private blockchains can function self-sufficiently or can be assimilated into other blockchains too. Organizations and enterprises typically utilize these. So, in private blockchains, the trust level among the parties involved is higher.

Application of Blockchain

1. Cryptocurrencies: We can integrate blockchain technology into numerous areas. The primary use of blockchains today is as a distributed ledger for cryptocurrencies, most particularly Bitcoin. A majority of cryptocurrencies utilize blockchain technology in recording transactions.

Although cryptocurrency was the first widespread application of blockchain technology, its importance has spread across several industries worldwide.

2. Smart contracts: Many private bodies and businesses interact to exchange products or services. These transactions usually come with conditions and terms which have to be agreed upon by all participants — this can be in the form of contracts or agreements. But the problem is that these paper-based contracts are susceptible to human hazards (fraud and errors), which tests the trust level between the parties involved, thereby raising the risk of doing business.

However, with blockchain-based smart contracts, these problems can be quickly addressed. At the same time, smart contracts are capable of performing the same purposes as paper-driven contracts. The distinguishing feature of smart contracts is that they are digital and self-executable. By being self-executable, specific rules in the contract's code are deployed and executed automatically.

As we now know, blockchain-based smart contracts are planned contracts that can be entirely or partly enforced or executed without human involvement. For example, one of the essential purposes of a smart contract is to automate escrow (a bond, deed, or document kept in the custody of a third party and taking effect only when a particular condition has been met). Moreover, because smart contracts are based on blockchain technology, the chances of moral hazards are reduced, and general use is optimized.

3. Banks: Most parts of the financial industry are applying distributed ledgers in banking at a fast rate. Because it can speed up back-office settlement systems, banks are invested in this technology to improve efficiency and lower the costs of their financial services.

4. Other uses: Blockchain technology can be leveraged to create a lasting, public, clear ledger system for collecting data on sales and monitoring digital usage and payments to content creators.

Remember

While many businesses are still reluctant to make blockchain the core of their business structure, the future of blockchain is bright. The original concept of dependable records and transferring power to users' hands have massive potentials; blockchain-based smart contracts are bound to revolutionize the system. And with the introduction of Ethereum, smart contracts have thrived in the blockchain ecosystem. Smart contracts can be used across various industries or situations — from financial agreements to crowdfunding to real estate property to even health insurance.

HOW BLOCKCHAIN IS CHANGING
THE FINANCIAL MARKET

Since its inception in 2008, blockchain technology has played a significant role in changing how business is done. While even in its early stages, this technology has managed to disrupt several sectors and industries. Its features, like transparency, immutability, and decentralization, have made it attractive for business domains and sectors worldwide. One sector that is making giant strides in harnessing the blockchain potential is the backing and finance sector.

Although there have been numerous challenges currently facing the rise of blockchain, it is agreed that it can transform the finance and banking sector by lowering service and labor costs. As a result, more and more financial executives are starting to reckon with blockchain technology across the globe. In addition, tech companies are always trying to leverage the system by spreading its application across other industries.

Because millions of dollars are constantly transferred from one part of the globe to another within 24 hours, the importance of blockchain is evident. Because the operation of our current banking and finance industry majorly relies on manual networks, the risk of human hazard (fraudulent activities and errors) is very high, which could result in a broken-down system of money management.

How it changes the banking sector20

In their bid to secure funds for customers, financial institutions require the services of any third parties. Because of the activities of these third parties, the cost of banking and transaction becomes more expensive. In fact, with too many individuals handling the processing and safekeeping of money, the probability of fraudulent activities and human error surges. However, with blockchain technology, all the hard work will be done by the system automatically. Hence, transactions will become more secure, and service costs will drop sharply. And most importantly, the overall customer experience improves significantly.

How some financial bodies are leveraging blockchain

While the financial world was skeptical about blockchain technology in its infancy, the story saw a drastic change today.

As blockchain technology continues to thrive across several industries, financial bodies become among the first people in line to take advantage of its benefits.

Top financial brands such as JB Morgan Chase, a US multinational investment bank, have steadfastly embraced the blockchain system. By developing Quorum, an internal division specializing in the research and execution of blockchain technology, the bank has become a significant player in this technology. A quorum is a smart contract and distributed ledger platform for organizations — it is capable of supporting quick transactions and outputs, thereby tackling the financial sector's significant problems.

Another top bank in the US, Bank of America, has already filed a patent document that discusses the execution of a permissioned blockchain to secure records and authenticate personal and personal business data. This system would permit only authorized parties to access the data and keep logs of every logging entry. Furthermore, this planned system would use blockchain technology to join several in-use data storage systems into a single body. This will produce a secured singular network that is capable of increasing the effectiveness and lowering the number of user data storage points

Goldman Sachs, another top finance player, is currently invested in researching and supporting a technology that enables distributed registry. By creating Circle, a well-sponsored cryptocurrency venture that is bound to make significant strides in the blockchain landscape, they plan to put an end to the considerable challenge of digital currency volatility. In so doing, they will make the financial industry more dependable with cryptocurrency options. And because Goldman Sachs aims to become the crypto kings of Wall Street, they are also in the process of creating a branded cryptocurrency trading desk that specially handles its digital trades.

Blockchain application in finance

Here are a few ways the adoption of blockchain will change things in the financial sector over the coming years:

1. Reduce fraudulent activities

When it comes to matters, the chance of fraud is very likely. More significantly, for a system that operates on a basic cash model, security is very crucial. And due to the sophistication of economic crimes today, several financial institutions and third parties (such as stock exchange and money transfer service providers) are liable to huge losses. This loss is caused by the dependence on a centralized database system used in managing funds and operating transactions. This system is highly susceptible to cyberattacks and system exploitation. Blockchain is a safer and tamper-proof technology that runs on a distributed database system for a more robust approach to prevent invasions and looting of hard-earned money. Because of the broadcast feature of blockchain, the likelihood of system failure is close to nil. Furthermore, because every transaction is kept in a block-based cryptographic form, it is hard to corrupt the system.

In addition, each block in the system is connected with a networking mechanism so that if one breach is found in one block, the other blocks will show the alteration in real-time. The breach can easily be noticed with this tracking feature, thus giving the cyber attacker no room to alter the entire system. With the implementation of a safer blockchain system, today's cyberattacks and crimes that plague the banking and finance industry will be significantly reduced.

2. Knowing your customer (KYC)

By complying with the rules of Know Your Customer (KYC) and Anti-Money Laundering (AML), financial bodies are always overwhelmed when carrying out all these time-consuming processes. Millions of dollars in expenditure comply with these regulations annually to prevent terrorist activities and money laundering. As a standard regulation, banks in the US have to upload their customers' KYC data to a central registry that can be used to check new or existing customer information. If blockchain is fully adopted in the system, the internal verification of each customer by a particular financial body or bank would be available to other institutions; therefore, starting the KYC does not have to start all over again. Because of blockchain technology, time would not be wasted in duplicating customer data. In addition, every update to customer data in one bank will reflect in real-time across all other financial institutions. Due to this, administrative work and the cost of compliance will be reduced across all departments.

3. The introduction of smart assets

Trade finance can become perplexing if asset transactions need to be logged with a specific timestamp and date. The fact is that global supply chains work with several components and entities that are being sold and purchased endlessly. And the paperwork needed in recording these details of supply and demand is even more complex. However, with the introduction of blockchain-based smart assets, records are stored in a digitized format and updated in real-time. A system running on a smart asset is not restricted to recording how items go from one point to another; it is also responsible for tracking where things come from and are delivered.

4. The rise of smart contracts

A smart contract is the future of the financial industry; its application will be crucial in improving banking processes and services. Because it enhances speed and simplifies intricate transaction processes, the ease of doing business is also enhanced. Smart contracts will likewise guarantee that information exchanged during any transaction is valid — as approval is only possible when all the agreed-upon conditions of the smart contract code are fulfilled. So, if the rules and conditions are available to all the participants associated with the transaction, the likelihood of error during the implementation period drops significantly.

5. Introduction of trade finance

In the backing industry, trade finance could well be one of the essential blockchain applications. With trade finance, participants associated with complex bank transactions can be onboarded on a blockchain network; likewise, information can be exchanged among banks, importers, exporters on a shared distributed ledger. Suppose the specific conditions of the agreement are fulfilled. In that case, by design, a smart contract will implement them by itself — with all involved participants capable of viewing and accessing every action carried out. Using blockchain technology, big names in the financial industry, like Barclays, have fruitfully implemented trade transactions that typically take seven to ten days in just four hours. In comparison to current systems, blockchain technology will significantly lower the overhead cost charges, such as the cost of ticketing and licensing.

HOW SMART CONTRACTS AFFECT EVERYDAY LIFE

The application of smart contracts to our everyday activities brings massive changes to the way business is done. Compared with traditional arrangements, smart contracts are significantly faster and easier to execute, allowing people and organizations to reorganize their workflows properly. In addition, with valuables, such as cash or property, being exchanged, these contracts offer the right amount of security and convenience.

Moreover, because smart contracts are built on blockchain technology, founded on openness, transparency is a crucial factor in these contracts. Every requirement, condition, or term of a transaction must be checked, agreed upon, and met by the involved participants, thus removing the likelihood of problems and disputes at the final stages of the terms and conditions. In addition, since the information is accessible to every party associated with the contract, the chances of miscommunication are lowered.

When drafting traditional contracts or documentation between two parties, the process takes days, as several third parties would most likely be involved to slow down the process. However, smart contract works on software code, running with the speed of the Internet. As a result, transactions are completed at lightning speed, saving hours, unlike any regular business procedure.

With speed also comes accuracy. The code of a smart contract is meticulous, requiring that all terms and conditions be met before it is eventually executed. If a term or condition were not found in the contract, it would not be enforced. Because of this fact, smart contracts beat traditional contracts in terms of precision and accuracy, as the chances of human error are lowered.

Safe and efficient, smart contracts function on an autonomous code, offering the most secure data encryption technology today. They are scalable in their reach to meet such top-quality safety measures, with thousands of transactions being executed without a glitch. As already established, the effectiveness of a contract is linked with its accessibility among all participants. All information is stored on the blockchain network and can be accessed anytime.

There is also the cost-effectiveness factor when thinking smart contracts. Parties do not have to involve or pay money to third parties or intermediaries other than regular contracts—no need to hire an attorney or even draft up a paper. In addition, since everything is coded, the paperless feature of smart contracts promotes convenience and seamlessness.

Finally, as a self-executing contract, smart contracts' security and openness encourage business trust and confidence. There is no room for manual alterations or human error. If all conditions are met, the contract executes itself automatically executes—reducing the need for courts, lawyers, or litigation.

Smart contracts applications

Whether you are purchasing services or products or applying for a new job, contractual agreements come to serve as evidence of such actions. Nevertheless, the intricate processes of regular contracts and paperwork are expensive, involve intermediaries, and are prone to manual errors.

As technology and digitization advance, smart contracts will allow these processes to be faster, more effective, and inexpensive. When third parties and intermediaries are eradicated, efficiency and effectiveness become the buzzword. Here is a list of sectors and industries that would benefit from this technology:

Insurance firms

Because of the absence of automation in insurance bodies, claims processing takes several months to execute. This could result in a massive dilemma for insurance agencies and their clients, who would be stuck in time constraints trying to get their money. Likewise, agencies will have to deal with inefficiency, poor customer satisfaction, and unwelcome administrative costs.

When smart contracts are implemented in such processes, they would be simplified and streamlined, as payment for claims would be automatically triggered when terms and conditions are met based on the agreement of the agency and client. For instance, if a natural disaster brought massive loss, smart contracts can be aptly executed so that clients can claim and use their funds in such difficult times. Moreover, any explicit information, such as the scope of loss inflicted, can be stored on the blockchain, and the amount of reparation can be consequently decided.

Internet of Things

With sensors, the Internet of things (IoT) technology is being deployed to link commonplace devices to the Internet to enhance system interconnectivity. These devices can also be connected to the blockchain network to monitor all the processes and products in the system. For instance, in a typical situation, consider the case of a customer who shipped the wrong order after buying a product online with a paying system linked to IoT and blockchain. Because of these technologies, the customer would know beforehand by tracking the product's location and information (from its warehouse exit to transportation, shipment, and doorstep delivery). As the system is fully automated, product tracking becomes an effortless affair. This is possible because system sensors, working alongside smart contracts, can form their nodes on the blockchain—therefore, the possession and location of any product can be tracked. The smart contract tracks the location status and updates it until the product is correctly delivered to the customer's front door.

Mortgage loans

A mortgage agreement is an intricate affair because many factors include out-goings, credit score, and mortgage income. For a mortgage loan to be execut-ed, all these factors must be thoroughly checked. Third parties and interme-diaries handle this process, which is often drawn-out and problematic for the loan applicant and the lender. However, if smart contracts are leveraged in such cases, the benefits would be astounding, as third-party systems and in-termediaries would be eradicated, removing the need for any drawn-out and problematic process. In addition, the relevant information is kept in a central location, which is available to all involved parties at all times.

1. Employment contracts: Smart contracts can also play an important role when drafting employment contracts. For traditional employment contracts, if the employee or employer does not meet the previously established condi-tions, there would be a breach in terms of the agreement. This could raise trust issues among the parties affected and even lead to more legal problems. How-ever, with smart contracts, such issues can be addressed effectively. When both parties share a smart contract, the terms and conditions are explicit and fair for all to see and review. The information on these contracts could include job responsibility, salary amount, work durations, etc. As soon as these trans-actions are logged on a smart contract, should any conflict arise, they can be easily accessed by the involved participants. This way, the employer-employ-ee relationship is greatly fostered.

In addition, smart contracts can be leveraged to make the wage payment pro-cess more effortless, as the relevant employee gets the agreed payment at the arranged time. Similarly, in the case of short-term employment, where the job candidate, employer, and recruitment agency are concerned, smart contracts can be deployed to show openness. The contract can prevent any recruitment agency from meddling with the agreement terms of the candidate after being hired by the organization. With the help of smart contracts, any alterations made in terms of the agreement can be easily discovered by all parties involved.

2. *Protecting copyrighted content.* In today's digital landscape, the meaning of content can be very expansive. It could range from audio and video files to handwritten documents. Hypothetically, once a piece of content is commercially released, the content's owner gets a royalty fee. Nevertheless, creative processes often demand several participants; therefore, all involved members are legally likely to receive royalty or payments for their work. However, in reality, this is not usually the case, as entitlement conflict among people can result in lengthy litigations, as there is no well-defined technique of settling the problems of claims and entitlement. But with smart contracts, confusion about royalties can be quickly resolved when the contribution of every party to the content is recorded on a blockchain network.

Thanks to the Internet, digital content can easily be replicated and circulated. Because of this, any person from across the globe can copy, duplicate, and use it without giving credits to the legitimate owner of the content. While we have copyright laws to safeguard owners of intellectual properties, according to collective worldwide standards, these laws are not adequately well explained. This means that a valid law in China might not be legally acceptable in the US.

Even when copyright laws are applied to intellectual contents, owners can forfeit control over their data and encounter monetary losses. With the help of blockchain technology, copyrights can be kept in the form of smart contracts, thereby enabling business automation, increasing online sales, and removing the risk of redistribution. From creators of content to their consumers, a smart contract provides copyright clarity for everyone. Once content owners register their work on the blockchain network, they will have tamper-proof evidence of their ownership. Moreover, because of the immutability feature of blockchain, every recorded entry on it can never be altered or deleted. Thus, the creator of the content will have complete control over content distribution and ownership.

3. *Supply chain:* Supply chain management requires the movement of products from the first stage to the last. As a core aspect of several companies, the proper operation of the supply chain is vital to any business. Because a supply chain demands a line of workers to be effective, it is not a one-person job and requires collaboration and some level of synchronization among workers. By leveraging smart contracts in the supply chain, ownership rights

of products can be recorded as they flow through the supply chain. Therefore, every worker in the network can track the location of the goods at any point in time. At each stage of their transfer to the end customer, the product can be monitored throughout the process of delivery. If an item is misplaced during this delivery process, a smart contract can be deployed to track it down. In addition, if any party does not meet up the conditions of the contract, it would be open for the entire network to detect, thereby ensuring transparency to the whole supply chain system.

Most times, supply chains are disadvantaged by paper-based systems. For example, forms have to pass through various channels before approval of any sort, thereby increasing the risk of loss and fraud. The blockchain cancels out this by providing a secure and handy digital platform to all participants on the chain, where payments and tasks are automated.

When it comes to managing drug supply, for instance, smart contracts can be helpful when deployed in healthcare. Once a drug (of known name and amount) is set to be transferred from the manufacturer. Then, a smart contract (stored with accurate data such as the supply quantity, drug information, etc.) can be deployed to the pharmacist. Such a contract will be tasked with managing entries throughout the length of the supply chain, monitoring every intermediate stop and channel.

4. *The electoral process:* While many professionals strongly claim that the voting system is complicated, smart contracts would resolve any concerns by offering a significantly more secure system. First, to decode and access ledger-secure votes, which smart contracts would provide, attackers would need massive computing powers, which nobody in the world possesses. Second, smart contracts would address the problem of low voter turnout, which is usually caused by the clumsy process of lining on queues, displaying identity, and filling forms. Finally, if smart contracts are introduced, online voting will be more secure, effective, and easy as voters cast their ballots en masse from the comfort of their homes.

No matter the level of security of the electoral process, criminal elements will still try to commit voter fraud. In addition, since our existing voting system functions on a manual process, the likelihood of manual errors is high. With smart contracts, however, the entire voting process can be automated, ensuring security and transparency of voters while upholding voter privacy and fair elections.

5. *Business Management*: Apart from being a trusted single ledger, the blockchain network also enhances workflow and communication because it runs on an automated system that is transparent and accurate. For example, business operations often carry out many deliberations before a decision is made; they also have to wait for approval before an external or internal issue can be addressed. However, if a blockchain ledger is used, the process can be streamlined, as it removes inconsistencies that usually happen with teams not working together. In addition, with such a ledger, everyone will be in sync, and the risk of expensive settlement delays or litigations is removed.

6. *Identity management*: As our society becomes more digitalized, financial transactions have gone mostly online: we enter our details and security password to access our money. However, in such a situation, the identity of the person withdrawing or using the funds cannot be ensured, no matter how secure the bank is. Once the password and username of accounts are hacked, money is life unsecured. However, if there is a system capable of managing personal identification online, security is considerably increased. Thankfully, the distributed ledger technology of blockchain technology provides sophisticated ways of private-public encryption, on which users can verify their identity and digitize their documents.

This exceptionally secure identity can be deployed when performing any transaction or interacting online on a mutual economy. This identity can help bridge several private and government organizations through blockchain-based general online identity solutions.

Remember

While smart contracts are still comparatively an emerging technology, they would soon spread like wildfire. From simple private agreements to government-sanctioned contracts, smart contracts will become a preferred alternative to traditional paper-based contracts. As a result, both buyers and sellers will track purchases in the supply chain and encourage trustworthiness.

Looking at the expensive cost of running through attorneys and government agencies when drafting agreements, smart contracts provide an inexpensive method free of the third-party system. In addition, as long the code is checked, the execution of smart contracts is automated, offering the chance of more streamlined routine processes and transactions. As technologies continue to evolve over the years to come, smart contracts will become widespread because of their apparent benefits.

ETHEREUM:

A PROGRAMMABLE BLOCKCHAIN FOR SMART CONTRACTS

We already know the role blockchain plays in making verifiable and distributed transactions possible. One significant instance of this is Bitcoin—the most well-known cryptocurrency in the world. Bitcoins, amounting to millions of dollars, make it one of the most important examples of how blockchain technology is viable.

Ethereum, on the other hand, is the answer to this question: what would happen if application or service providers in the world vanished today? Ethereum is a platform capable of running decentralized applications—applications that do not depend on central servers.

A recap of the blockchain technology

A blockchain is a data store that is verifiable and distributed. It functions by combining public-key cryptography with the unique model of proof-of-work. Every transaction performed on the blockchain network must be approved by the legitimate owner of the traded asset. When new coins (assets) are formed, they are given to the owner. Sequentially, this owner can prepare recent transactions and send those coins to other people by just inserting the public key of the new owner into the trade, then approving the transaction with a personal private key. In doing so, a verifiable link of transactions is generated; each new transaction and the new owner will point to the initial transaction and the preceding owner. Blockchain technology deploys the proof-of-work model to manage these transactions and avoid the double-spending issues (duplicating or falsifying coins).

The proof-of-work system generates a cost for assigning transactions in a specific order and including them in the blockchain. These assignments of transactions are referred to as blocks. Each block is pointing to a preceding block in the chain, hence the term "blockchain." My ensuring blocks are expensive to create and ensuring each new block points to the previous block, any potential hacker trying to change the history of transactions as shown in the blockchain has to pay the cost of each block changed. Since blocks link to preceding blocks, changing old blocks demands paying the price for every block after it, therefore ensuring alteration to old blocks is highly expensive. Thus, a blockchain raises the trouble of changing the blockchain by guaranteeing the cost of generating blocks is founded on a computational basis.

Simply put: to generate new blocks, a specific amount of CPU power needs to be exhausted. Because CPU power relies on technological advancement, it is challenging for anyone malicious attacker to gather enough CPU power in outspending the entire network. A feasible attack against a blockchain-based network often needs one body to control over 50 percent of the total CPU power of such a network. Thus, the more extensive the network, the more challenging it gets for an attack to be carried out.

However, as already established, the application of blockchain spans beyond simple transactions. Transactions go beyond sending assets from one party to another. This very process can be referred to as a pretty simple program: the sender generates a computation (transaction), which can only be carried out if the receiver provides, at some future time, the appropriate inputs. The correct information would be the receiver's proof of ownership when it comes to traditional monetary transactions. Simply put, a receiver can spend the received coins only if they can prove rightful ownership of those coins. Although it sounds a bit unnatural, it is not. For example, when performing wire transfers, some credentials or authentication processes are needed to prove the ownership of the account. For some online banking services, this could just be a password and username. At the onsite bank branch, it could be a debit card or some ID card. These processes are often coded into the banking system. However, with blockchain, this is not necessary.

Note that for Bitcoin transactions, just like bank processes, senders (by deploying a public key to verify identities) can transfer coins to the receiver: this is the traditional "Point A to Point B" monetary transaction, where ID cards are replaced with private and public keys. Nevertheless, this does not stop the further application of blockchain. For instance, timestamped and immutable messages can be stored on the blockchain forever. The older these messages become, the more difficult it is to change them.

While the blockchain concept was conceptualized from cryptocurrency-based research, the blockchain has a vast array of other powerful applications. The job of blockchain is basically to encode an only factor: state transitions. Once a sender transfers a coin (Bitcoin) to another party, the universal state of the blockchain is altered. For example, account X held 100 coins before, but account X is void now, and account Y has 100 coins. In addition, the blockchain offers a cryptographically safe method of carrying out these state transitions. In simpler terms, any outside party of the transaction can verify the state of the blockchain; likewise, any state transition started by users on the blockchain network can be carried out in a verifiable and secure way.

One excellent explanation of blockchain is a never-stopping computation: new data and instructions are tapped from a pool of unverified transactions. Each result is stored on the blockchain, which creates the computation state. Thus, any single picture of the blockchain is its computational state then.

In some significant way, every software system works with state transitions. Note that blockchain-based state transitions are not restricted to sending coins.

The decentralized computational feature of blockchain can be applied to several other things. The Ethereum network comes in: a blockchain capable of carrying out any computation as an aspect of a transaction.

Although the landscapes of transactions (between two users) and cryptocurrency are buzzing nowadays when it comes to blockchain, we can deploy this technology's secure and distributed computations to other applications.

Moving past Bitcoin: first-generation decentralized apps

While Bitcoin seems to be the standout feature of blockchain, the technology's applications are much more than just being used to spend digital currencies. In reality, there are several hundred ways blockchain technologies can be deployed today. In addition, just like email is to the Internet, so is Bitcoin to blockchain—a large data store or electronic platform where applications are built. One of which is currency. Before now, creating blockchain applications demanded an intricate understanding of mathematics, cryptography, coding, and some relevant skills. However, advances have made things easier. Until this time, never-before-imagined applications—such as trading, regulatory compliance, digitally recorded property assets, and electronic voting—are now keenly been created and used with more incredible speed, security, and efficiency. Ethereum is opening up new possibilities because it provides developers the tools to build decentralized applications.

Note: a decentralized application is an application executed by several users on a decentralized network. They are created in such a way to circumvent every point of failure. Users, who provide computing power for the execution of this application, are rewarded with tokens. Bitcoin, for instance, is an example of a decentralized application because it offers its users a peer-to-peer electronic fund system that allows the payment of Bitcoins online. Since decentralized applications consist of code running on a blockchain network, they are not controlled by any central body or individual.

Ethereum — basics

Simply put, Ethereum is a blockchain-based open software platform that allows developers to create and use decentralized applications. Similar to Bitcoin, Ethereum is a blockchain network that is public and distributed. While the two have some substantial distinctions between them, the most vital difference to know is that Ethereum and Bitcoin differ considerably in capability and purpose. Bitcoin provides one specific application of blockchain technology: the peer-to-peer electronic fund system, which permits the payments of Bitcoin. Therefore, while the Bitcoin-based blockchain is deployed in tracking ownership of cryptocurrency (Bitcoins), the Ethereum-based blockchain concentrates on executing the programming code of all decentralized applications.

Since decentralized applications run on the blockchain, Ethereum enjoys the qualities of blockchain. From immutability (third-party entities cannot alter data) to tamper-proof (applications are designed on a consensus network, where censorship is prohibited), to security (securing applications from fraud and cyberattacks, thanks to the usage of cryptography and the absence of any central point of failure), to zero downtime (application cannot be turned off and powered down).

Ether

While Ethereum introduces broad computations to the blockchain, it stills deploys "coins." Its coin is referred to as "Ether." In the Ethereum-based blockchain, rather than mining for Bitcoins, miners labor to be rewarded with Ether. Ether is a form of cryptocurrency that powers the Ethereum-based platform. Apart from being used as tokens for transactions, Ether can be deployed by developers (of decentralized application) to pay for transaction services and fees on the Ethereum platform.

"Gas" is the amount of token deployed to pay miners who store transactions in blocks; the execution of all smart contracts needs a specific amount of gas to be embedded in it — for enticing miners to include such contract in the blockchain.

How smart contracts connect with Ethereum

Ethereum-based blockchain has some unique abilities. One is that it can be used to create smart contracts — a self-executing contract that handles the execution, administration, performance, and payment associated with the contract. As we already know, a smart contract is computer code that can simplify the exchange of cash, shares, property, intellectual content, or any valuables. Because smart contracts run on blockchain technology, such contracts work like an autonomous computer program, capable of executing themselves automatically under certain met conditions. Furthermore, by running on the blockchain, smart contracts perform their programmed instruction with any likelihood of third-party meddling, fraud, downtime, or censorship.

Although all blockchains are capable of processing code, most are highly restricted in their capabilities. Ethereum, however, is significantly wide-ranging in its uses. Moreover, instead of granting only a list of regional operations, Ethereum permits developers to build any function they desire. In other words, Ethereum-based blockchain can be used in making thousands of applications with beneficial uses.

The Ethereum Virtual Machine

Before the conceptualization of Ethereum, blockchain application was very limited to a set of operations. For instance, Bitcoin and other forms of cryptocurrency were designed solo work as a peer-to-peer method of transacting with digital currencies. However, soon developers of the blockchain network were facing an issue. To either grow the number of functions provided by Bitcoin and other forms of applications, which is severely time-consuming and challenging, or create a new blockchain platform and, as well, a new platform. Spotting this issue, Vitalik Buterin — creator of Ethereum — came up with a new method.

The Ethereum Virtual Machine (EVM), a significant invention of Ethereum, is Turing-complete software running on the Ethereum network. As long as there are enough computer memory and time, this software lets users run any program, despite the programming language of that program; the EVM permits the seamless and influential building of blockchain applications. Moreover, rather than having to create an entirely new blockchain for each new application, Ethereum allows the creation of thousands of various applications on a singular platform.

Note that by leveraging Ethereum, any centralized services can become decentralized. For example, consider each third-party system spread across the various sectors and industries worldwide, from apparent services like bank loans to the less flashy intermediate services involved with regulatory compliance, voting systems, title registries, etc. With centralization gone, ease is raised, and the cost of doing business is reduced.

Decentralized Autonomous Organizations (DAO)

Ethereum can be deployed to create Decentralized Autonomous Organizations (DAO). A DAO is an organization that is entirely decentralized and autonomous — without one single leader. A DAO is operated by a programming code and runs on a collective of smart contracts recorded on the Ethereum-based blockchain. The code is created to substitute the structure and rules of traditional organizations, removing the requirement for centralized authority. The DAO is owned by every party that buys tokens; however, tokens serve as donations that grant each party voting rights rather than each token representing ownership or equity shares.

A DAO comprises one or more contracts; it could be financed by a collective of people who share a goal. Its functions are fully transparent and independent of any human interference, even its original designers. Apart from covering its operating cost, the lifespan of a DAO is dependent on its service usefulness to its customer base.

Shortcomings of decentralized applications

Despite its numerous benefits, decentralized applications still have their faults. Since smart contract code is man-written, smart contracts are only as effective as those who write them. Oversights or coded bugs can cause unwanted nefarious actions to take place. Once a code error is exploited, the only way to counter exploitations or attacks is to obtain a network consensus to rewrite the original code. This practice opposes the nature of blockchain that proclaims immutability. Likewise, any action performed by a central body could raise challenging questions about an application's decentralized nature.

Using Solidity to Build Ethereum Smart Contract

The process of creating a smart contract requires some simple steps. Your reasons for building one can vary: from understanding how it works to building your dApp (decentralized application) or launching an ICO (Initial Coin Offering).

Note: ICO is a cryptocurrency-based equivalent to an Initial Public Offering (IPO) in the mainstream investment world.

No matter your intentions, understanding the inner workings of a smart contract is very important. In some years' time, the Ethereum platform has a great potential to create dApps that could alter how we communicate in cyberspace. Although Ethereum uses smart contracts that function as a regular blockchain transaction, such contracts produce a line of condition(s) that must be satisfied before an action(s) is carried out. Smart contracts are deployed in multi-signature wallets, blind auctions, crowdfunding, voting, and many other things.

A simple breakdown of the smart contract:

John possesses a steel business in the US, and Matt is his China-based metal supplier. Both men have an excellent business relationship. Their decade-long relationship is built on trust. Both are enjoying business growth, especially John, who sells out steel blocks every time. John then drafts a contract when his steel inventory reaches a specific limit; he automatically orders Matt for 500 Ibs of steel blocks at 50 Ether per ton. Matt approves of this arrangement and takes John's Ether payment immediately. After that, matt starts supplying to fulfill John's order. Matt can then trade off his Ether for Yuan at an online exchange website for a small fee, and he will cash out instantly. Whether Matt chooses to exchange is Ether or hold on to it is his decision. Whatever his decision, he can immediately reinvest his capital.

Now both men are happy with the arrangement. Customarily, without a smart contract, John has to reach out to his bank and attempt a wire transfer to Matt's Chinese bank. It usually takes about two days for this process to be completed — even so, Matt would endure a waiting time of some days before the bank clears his transfer. Besides, John will be charged a transfer fee by his bank to send funds to Matt. In such a case, money and time are wasted. If that is not enough, both men need to battle the foreign exchange issues, converting US Dollars to Chinese Yuan.

Learning the basics

Note: a little programming knowledge would be helpful in this section

To build a smart contract, we must start from scratch. Before we begin using a contract, it is crucial to understand the basics. More crucially, the role the Ethereum platform plays in all this.

Note: if you come across a problem with a program at any point, consider launching the program as administrator. Just right-click it and select Run as administrator on your computer.

Creating an Ethereum node

An Ethereum node (or client) is a device (software) that can run blockchain — the Ethereum protocol. Though nodes can customarily run on laptops and desktops, mobile platforms are currently being developed. When you run the Ethereum node, you can link up with other nodes on the network, thereby getting straight admission to the blockchain. Hence, we start deploying smart contracts, sending transactions, and mining blocks — all on the blockchain network.

Nodes are written in Python, C++, and Go (Go Ethereum/Geth). In this guide, we will be working with Go — the most widely used of three. Understand that downloading Geth means downloading the complete Ethereum blockchain, which is about 35 Gigabytes of your hard drive's storage.

1) To install Geth, go to the Go Ethereum site to download

2) Then download Geth's latest Windows version (as of the publication: version 1.8.7) — ensure it is the 64-bit version.

3) After downloading, tap the installer and select I Agree.

4) Ensure to check the Geth box and select Next.

5) To complete the installation, you will be asked to choose the destination folder. The default folder is C:\Program Files\Geth.

6) After installation is completed, close the installer.

7) Open a command prompt. For easier input of command lines, you can download a command-line tool like Git Bash; during its installation, ensure to add Git Bash to your PATH variable). Next, type "cd C:\Program Files\Geth" to go to the Geth directory

8) Type "Geth" to initiate synchronization to the Ethereum blockchain. Since this is a first-time synchronization, the whole blockchain from every peer is downloaded. Depending on your internet speed, the download time could take a while.

After the downloading is done, you can begin to run on your own Ethereum node.

Creating a private Ethereum network

Once you get admission to the Ethereum network through your node, you create a personal private server to build and use smart contracts. Understand that, for a private Ethereum network, these contracts cannot be used on the Ethereum blockchain, but instead, they can be deployed on your blockchain.

Building the first block in your blockchain: (genesis.json) — aka the genesis block

1. Set up a new desktop folder and name it "Private Chain." In this same folder, open a command prompt (press shift + right-click and select open command window here) and type "Mkdir chain data" to set up a data directory subfolder named "chain data."

2. Then, you will have to build and store your genesis.json block in your Private Chain folder. This genesis block will be deployed in initializing your private network and storing data in chain data — the folder for data directory.

3. Open a notepad on your desktop. Copy the below code, paste it on your notepad, and save the file as "genesis.json" in your Private Chain folder.

```
{

 "coinbase"   : "0x0000000000000000000000000000000000000001",

 "difficulty" : "0x20000",

 "extraData"  : "",

 "gasLimit"   : "0x2fefd8",

 "nonce"      : "0x0000000000000042",

 "mixhash"    : "0x00000000000000000000000000000000000000000000000000000000
0000000000000",

 "parentHash" : "0x00000000000000000000000000000000000000000000000000000000
00000000000000",

 "timestamp"  : "0x00",

 "alloc": {},

 "config": {
```

«chainId»: 15,

"homesteadBlock": 0,

«eip155Block»: 0,

«eip158Block»: 0

}

}

4. Next, you will have to start up your private network (located in the chaindata directory) by deploying your genesis.json file. Now ask Geth to always put the data guide in the "chaindata" subfolder and also tell Geth where it can find the genesis.json file. Note: ensure genesis.json is never placed in the chain data subfolder; it is only recognized in the Private Chain folder.

To do this, open a command line, type the command below into the command line, which points to the Private Chain folder.

geth --datadir=./chaindata/ init ./genesis.json

5. Ensure that the genesis state was written successfully.

6. Next, start up Geth and link it your personal private chain. Here, the geth. ipc endpoint socket connection and port 30303 opens.

geth --datadir=./chaindata

Anytime Geth is started up, the IPC endpoint opens — this is deployed for processing connections between Geth and programs such as Mist, Ethereum Wallet, and MetaMask. Alternatively, the IPC endpoint is deployed to open the Geth Javascript API console. More of these will be explained as we proceed.

Now, you have created your personal private Geth network.

Meaning of MetaMask

MetaMask functions as an Ethereum wallet as well as a browser. Via MetaMask, one can begin interacting with smart contracts and dApps online without needing to install software or download the blockchain. MetaMask can be used as an extension exclusively on your Chrome browser for depositing Ether or creating a wallet.

Visit this link to download MetaMask.

The Mist browser

Mist can be referred to as an electron application—this means that it is a desktop hybrid application that features a web interface. This feature makes the browser application smoother and faster. Mist is an important and powerful browser because when it launches, a Geth node will run in the background as well, triggering an instant access to the Ethereum-based blockchain network. However, since you are building a smart network, Mist is not needed to access the default Geth node. Instead, you should run your node on your private network.

Ethereum Wallet

Ethereum Wallet is operation in the Mist browser that can exclusively access just one dApp: the wallet app. Written only in Javascript and HTML code and running within the Mist browser, Ethereum Wallet deploys web3.js in managing your accounts. Click here to download the Ethereum Wallet.

❖ To download the Mist browser to can connect to your private network, go the Mist page to find the latest version for download.

❖ Select I Agree after opening up the installer.

❖ Select Next to choose your default download path: C:\Program Files\Mist (default)

❖ Ensure the blockchain data is stored in the default path under \ Roaming\Ethereum, and then select Install.

❖ Connect Mist your own private network

After setting up your private network with the genesis block, you can set up a command line in your "Private Chain" folder to ask Geth to link up with your datadir. Do so by typing the command into your command prompt:

geth --datadir=./chaindata/

Geth will then begin to run.

Next, open your Mist browser to activate your geth. ipc endpoint. Now the Mist browser will automatically connect to your private network. Ensure Mist is connected by checking if the Private-Net sign is visible in the upper-right window of the Mist window. Do not bother with the Looking for peers sign since you are on your own network and do not have to link up with other peers.

Fundamentals of the Mist browser

1. On the upper-left corner is the tool bar. Go to the Develop tab, under it, is the grayed-out Ethereum Node — showing that you are not connected to Geth since you are running your network. Just like the Chrome browser, you can navigate to the Developers Tools beneath the Develop tab.

2. On the upper-left side of the Mist browser, like any browser, you can access several open tabs. To open the Ethereum Wallet, click on the green box. This wallet is a distributed application (dApp) that enables your smooth interaction with the Go Ethereum's JavaScript interface.

3. Via https://wallet.ethereum.org/, you are linked up to the Ethereum network. With the Mist browser, you can now watch contracts or deploy contracts, send Ether, as well as view past transactions,

4. Navigate down the Wallets tab, to add new accounts, view your accounts, import or create wallet contracts (such as multi-signature wallet contracts or single owner accounts), and likewise see old transactions.

5. To set up an account, select Add Account (which means add wallet), Create new account, and then input a strong password. Select OK to complete the setup of your wallet.

Beneath the Send tab, you can transfer Ether from wallet to wallet or from wallet to contract. After selecting Send, you have a choice of setting the gas (transaction fee). All transactions need some gas level to encourage processing. You can adjust the amount of gas to pay — this depends on how quick you need the transaction sanctioned and processed by the blockchain network.

Now, beneath the Contracts tab, you can start watching current contracts and past tokens while deploying new contracts. It is with this tab, you can start creating and deploying your Hello World! contract.

You can likewise watch past tokens and contracts. To interact with a previously used to contract, select Watch Contracts, input the contract ABI (application binary interface), contract address, and contract name. If you want to watch or spend ERC-20 tokens (Ethereum-generated tokens on the blockchain), enter the token symbol, name, and contract address.

Bonus: Navigate to the Explorer tab and click it. This triggers a new web page in the browser. Select connects on the top-right corner to connect with your browser with your wallet—this is a Web 3.0 connection. Now you are able to go to any Ethereum-based distributed applications (dApps) and work with them with your wallet. For instance, you can interact with dApps on sites like this. Since you are on a private network, you can easily connect your wallet your browser. However, you should note that you do not have any Ether yet; therefore, your interaction with these distributed applications will be limited. To enjoy a complete experience, you will have to link up with the Ethereum network and transfer Ether into your wallet. But this does not mean you cannot browse these dApps right now.

The function of Web3.js

Mist is simply a browser, but it is capable of connecting your wallet to a browser and interacting with the Ethereum blockchain. Mist can do all these thanks to a browser injection called Web3.js library; this lets you interact with Ethereum nodes on it while transacting with blockchain-deployed smart contracts.

Keep in mind

While all these may seem too much at first, keep in mind that they will make much sense as you proceed. Now you will have to interact with Remix, use Solidity to write your first smart control, deploy it via Mist, and work with it.

Remix IDE

Remix is a popular, open source tool (also a web browser) used in writing Solidity contracts. Remix IDE (integrated development environment) can likewise be used to test, debug, and deploy smart contracts.

Solidity, on the other hand, is a contract-based programming language that can be used to write smart and implement smart contract on several blockchain platforms.

Now it is down to writing code. Although you can note code straight into the Mist browser, writing your first Solidity code is easier with the Remix IDE. This is because Remix is equipped with some features that give it a more detailed development for beginners starting out with small-sized contracts.

The features of Remix are:

❖ Integrated debugger (call stack, call data, monitoring variables, and stage by stage instructions)

❖ Warnings to check for overlapping variable names, constant function, gas cost, and unsafe code.

❖ Integrated deployment and testing environment.

❖ Highlights error and syntax.

❖ Functions with Web3 objects injection.

❖ Can be deployed straight to Mist or MetaMask

❖ Static analysis.

To access Remix, visit the official website. In the center of the webpage, you will be able to see the space to enter your code. On the top-left screen corner, you will find some file option for "creating new files," "adding local files, "copying all files to another instance, "connecting to local host," and "publishing open files to anonymous Github Gist."

On the top-left screen corner, you will some tabs you can choose from. Your Compile tab helps you in compiling your contract once it is completed (by default: it auto-compiles). When you select Details, you will see a list of some contracts' details like Web3 deployment code of the contract, ABI, bytecode, and metadata.

The Support, Analysis, Debugger, and Settings tabs are all-important, so endeavor to familiarize yourself with them. Now, this guide is particularly interested in the Run tab. So When you select the Run tab, the contract settings listed below appears:

Environment: You can plug Remix to three forms of environment: Injected Web3, Web3 Provider, and JavaScript VM. Both Injected Web3 and Web3 Provider environments execute only on external tools such as Mist or MetaMask. However, JavaScript VM environment can enable execution both on the Remix browser as well as on the Mist browser.

Account: Remix offers five separate accounts preloaded with Ether (100), which can be utilized when developing your contract

Gas limit: Enter, the limit for the amount of gas (transaction feed), linked to your contract.

Gas Price: Enter the amount of gas needed for the processing of the contract.

Value: Enter the amount of Ether linked to the contract.

Going on Solidity

If you have some knowledge of Javascript, you can easily spot its similarities with Solidity. Similar to Javascript, Solidity is a contract-based, high-grade language created to work with the Machine (EVM). It is a statical code written to support intricate user-based types, libraries, inheritance, and many other things.

To create a Hello World! contract, set up a state variable named "counter" and give it an initial value of 5. Next, set up a function capable of increasing your state variable by 1, a function capable of decreasing the variable by 1, a function capable of returning your counter, and finally a function capable of destroying the contract.

Your source code version should be the first piece of code to enter into Remix. As of now, the latest version of Solidity compactible with Mist is version 0.4.16. Begin by writing this version as the heading of your contract:

pragma solidity ^0.4.16;

Pragma is a keyword that tells the complier (Remix) how the source code should be treated.

For more on Solidity, visit their website.

States and functions

When broken down to its most basic entities, a smart contract is simply a collection of data (its states) and code (it's functions) that tally to a certain blockchain-based contract address.

For instance, the line uint256 counter is used to set up the variable counter of type uint256 (unsigned {meaning exclusively positive – neither positive nor negative} integer of 256 bits). It can then be seen as just one slot in the database, which can be retrieved when you call the code function managing the database. You can even enter a value for the variable counter and also set the types as uint256.

uint256 counter = 5;

Because they are basically function-free, state variables will be used in the first few lines of your contract. After setting your variable counter as uint256 and your value as 5, you can move to the next step.

Next: command a function to increase the value of your counter by 1. To do so, you will have to set up a function and command it to "add" 1 to the counter.

function add() public {

  counter++;

}

After using the function "add()," your counter will now get a value of 6.

Setting up the contract

To set up your "Hello World!" contract, you must first create a contract named:

pragma solidity ^0.4.16;

contract HelloWorld {

}

Now, you can introduce the earlier mentioned counter state variable and assign it as an unsigned integer of 256 bit. Then you can set it to a value of 5.

pragma solidity ^0.4.16;

contract HelloWorld {

  uint256 counter = 5;

}

Now set up two functions under this assigned state variable.

- First function to increase the counter by 1

- Second function to decrease the counter one

pragma solidity ^0.4.16;

contract HelloWorld {

uint256 counter = 5; //state variable we assigned earlier

function add() public { //increases counter by 1

counter++;

}

function subtract() public { //decreases counter by 1

counter--;

}

}

In the above code, both functions are assigned to a modifier named public. Because Solidity understands two types of function calls—external calls that create a real Ethereum Virtual Machine call and internal calls that do not (aka "message call), they are four visibility forms for state and functions variables. Functions are stated as being private, internal, public, or external; public is the set default. Although if you did not include it, Remix would send a warning notification that says that you did not specify your visibility and thereby it will default to public. Still, you should form the habit of always entering your function visibility. This will grand you better understanding of the contract settings as you evaluate your code.

Contingent your called function, you can always alter your state variable. However, you still require a function capable of outputting the value of the counter. To perform this, create a function named "getCounter()" which will be returning the counter. Note that is action is read-only; therefore, tell the function that you want to return a constant. In addition, if you want to return a state variable, tell your function the type you want to return. Here, as previously mentioned, you should return a uint256.

```solidity
pragma solidity ^0.4.16;

contract HelloWorld {

uint256  counter = 5; //state variable we assigned earlier

function add() public { //increases counter by 1

counter++;

}

function subtract() public { //decreases counter by 1

counter--;

}

function getCounter() public constant returns (uint256 ) {

return counter;

}

}
```

Note: Although when you call functions on the Ethereum, gas is used, however, when you return a constant function, no gas is spent.

Now you have a contact that lets you alter the value of your global variable counter. With this setup, you are capable of increasing your variable counter by 1, decreasing it by 1, and returning it whenever you choose to.

Testing your contract

From here, your code is stored in Remix. Beneath, the Compile tab, ensure that "Auto-compile" is set default. Navigate to the Run tab. Ensure the default settings as set the environment to JavaScript VM, your account has been picked, 3000000 gas limit has been set, and that your gas value and price are set to 0. Beneath the Run tab, select "Create." After doing this, you will be able to view the details of your contracts and the three functions you have created in your code:

• "add"

- "subtract"

- "getCounter"

In addition, you can view the state variable in its assigned value of 5. To raise your counter by 1, select "add." To call your recently changed counter, select "getCounter." Hence, you value will be updated to 6. You can as well repeat the process for the "subtract" feature. After all this is done, you have now successfully created your own contract.

Deploy the contract in Mist

After testing and confirming your code in Remit, open Mist (ensure it is linked to the Private Network), consider deploying your code on your private network. Go, the Mist's Ethereum Wallet, enter the Contracts tab. Click on "Deploy New Contract," and paste your code from Remix into the source code box. Of course, you need to have Ether in your wallet to proceed. You can mine for Ether on your private network through a miner. This can be done via Geth JavaScript console.

Open a new command prompt window that points to your private network folder (C:/users/name/desktop/private network) and type "geth attach" and press "enter." This action will generate a Geth JavaScript console where you can directly input commands into Geth. To initialize Ether mining, type "miner.start();". Now the console will return to "null," showing that mining has started. Check out your Ethereum Wallet on Mist to see boosts of 5 Ether continually added. To end the miner whenever you want, enter "miner. stop();" in the console.

Note: This self-generated Ether is fake: it can only be deployed in your private Ethereum network and cannot be used to make any transaction on the main Ethereum network.

 Now navigates the Contracts tab, and then move to «Deploy new contract.» Also, ensure your code is in the box allocated for source code. On the right side of that box, select «Hello World.» Next, select «DEPLOY» to deploy your contract. You will be prompted to enter your password. Once you have done so, go back to the Wallets tab and move down to «Latest Transactions» where you can see your recently deployed contract. You will likewise observe that the contract is showing 0 of 12 confirmations, as it is stagnant in «Creating contract» stage.

This is happening because your contract has not been completed set up, as their no available miners on your network to confirm your recently deployed contract. Begin to mine again via the Geth JavaScript console (miner.start();). After you initiate mining again, the confirmation numbers will begin to rise, ultimately deploying your contract completely.

Next, select the contract name — from here, you can execute contract functions, obtain the contracts interface (ABI), produce a scannable QR code, copy the contract address, and send Ether to the contract.

Your "Hello World" contract will display your "getCounter()" function with the counter state variable of 5. Navigate to "Select function" and choose either to "subtract" or "add" function. Once chose, click on "execute." Remember you are on a private network so you have to run your own miner to authenticate every transaction. After executing a "subtract" or "add" function, the contract should return a value of 4 or 6 respectively. This shows that you now have a functioning smart contract on your private Ethereum blockchain network capable of interacting with Mist.

Add the self-destruct function

As already established, once a contract is deployed, it is formally included to the Ethereum blockchain; therefore, any part with the contract address is capable of interacting with the contract, to some certain extent. However, what if you, the contract owner, decides to delete it from the blockchain network. Thankfully, Solidity provides a seamless way of ending your contract. This is done by performing a self-destruct operation. Once a contract is self-destructed, all the residual Ether kept in the contract address is transferred to an assigned target and the contract is deleted.

Although you have the option of deleting the contract, you have to ensure that such action can only be carried out by you — the contract creator. It is very dangerous if you do not give self-destruct rights to a specific party.

To begin this process, you need to initially tell your contract who the contract owner is — this is the "msg.sender." Now enter the state variable owner as msg.sender. Since the msg.sender is linked to an address, you have to tell Solidity that the state variable needs to be given an address.

pragma solidity ^0.4.16;

contract HelloWorld {

  uint256 counter = 5; //state variable we assigned earlier

address owner = msg.sender; //set owner as msg.sender

....

}

You can call the self-destruct function "kill". Then set up a provisional statement to make sure the party performing the kill function is, in fact, the creator. To ask the contract to transfer Ether back to contract's owner after self-destruction, "selfdestruct(owner);".

```solidity
pragma solidity ^0.4.16;

contract HelloWorld {

  uint256 counter = 5; //state variable we assigned earlier

  address owner = msg.sender; //set owner as msg.sender

  function add() public { //increases counter by 1

    counter++;

  }

  function subtract() public { //decreases counter by 1

    counter--;

  }

  function getCounter() public constant returns (uint256) {

    return counter;

    }

  function kill() public { //self-destruct function,

    if(msg.sender == owner) {

    selfdestruct(owner);

      }

}
```

Now you can return to Mist and recreate a fresh contract with an added "kill()" function. Note that once a contract is destroyed, its Ether will be transferred to an assigned contract. However, to ensure your contract receives Ether, you must add a function for fallback to its code. Without a fallback option, a contract cannot receive Ether from another self-destructed contract.

To initiate a fallback option, you must have precisely one nameless function in your code. It is this unnamed function you will tag as "payable." To do this, place this function below the ""kill()" function :

function () public payable {

  }

Now your contract can receive Ether from wallets with contract addresses.

THE FUTURE OF SMART LEGAL CONTRACTS

Smart contracts are designed to be transparent, accurate, self-governing, and self-sufficient. The potentials and application of a smart contract will make it a powerful tool for executing and performing transactions and legal agreements. However, there are technological and legal challenges that need to be tackled first. For example, smart contracts (and smart legal ones) have to be legally enforceable in court. While many blockchain users believe the law should not play a role in smart contract disputes, this is not necessarily true. As long as a transaction takes place, smart contracts must be made to be legally enforced and binding.

Despite the many benefits of smart contracts, blockchain technology is still relatively in its infancy, and it would take time for it to become fully mainstream. Therefore, before we embrace this technology, we must clarify its regulatory and legal aspects.

Of course, when it comes to blockchain technology, we are not there yet. We do not yet have a blockchain network with adequate interconnections between financial assets and systems registers. But, on the basic level, there is a certainty to code. It is a pre-planned assembly of inputs to generate the desired output. Compared with traditional language, it is free from the traps of sub-text and ambiguity.

The certainty of a smart contract is its significant advantage. If the code is functioning, there is no room for misunderstanding. Still, many attorneys would argue that, from time to time, intentional ambiguity and the option of qualifying a condition are essential tools for a lawyer.

Ethereum is a front-running platform mainly created for smart contracts. While more popular cryptocurrencies, like Bitcoin, can store and transfer value, Ethereum can carry data in arguments forms—this means you can program the platform to perform certain actions once some specific conditions are satisfied. Therefore, you can program a contract to self-execute, as the platform can send funds once certain conditions are met.

In theory, if there is sufficient time, the platform will ultimately solve all computable problems. Nevertheless, realistically, the performance of this platform is contingent upon memory and network speed. While smart contract technology has enjoyed many advances, the technology is still developing. Before it can be fully adopted into the mainstream, usability, centralization risk, and scalability issues need to be addressed. The scalability issue comes up because the technology depends on network speed. More complex transactions need a much faster network speed, which only a few people have access to.

This could result in centralization risk, as power is majorly available in the hands of a few. Furthermore, such power concentration could result in a group of malicious bodies conspiring together to authorize fraudulent transactions. Lastly, these so-called smart contracts are still basically written in code and readable by the traditional attorney. Therefore, special tools will have to be created to bridge this gap of usability.

In the end, as smart contract grows, it will disrupt several sectors. Main sectors like healthcare, manufacturing, real estate, government, and financial services have started testing this innovative technology. Given enough time, complete implementation is bound to occur. Attorneys need to be up to date about how this technology can affect their clients. Transactional attorneys may need to study the technical areas of a smart contract to make sure it follows the client's goals and wishes. In years to come, litigation lawyers may not have to bother with a paper-based contract; instead, they want to know the meaning of the code.

ABOUT THE AUTHOR

"Happiness is not something ready-made. It comes from your own actions."

Dennis Roßbach is an Expert in Procurement and a serial entrepreneur in E-Commerce and Blockchain Technology. As a speaker and Advisor, he has a vast global network helping companies to grow and prosper. He is an open-minded and helpful world traveler. Born in 1989 in Germany, he finished school and his vocational training. He worked for companies such as Accenture and Rolls-Royce before he founded his first company. The SYBX Group was founded in Germany and had its headquarter in Luxembourg.

For more details, visit www.sybxgroup.lu

or get in touch via moien@sybxgroup.lu